TWAYNE'S WORLD AUTHORS SERIES
A Survey of the World's Literature

FRANCE

Maxwell A. Smith
Guerry Professor of French, Emeritus
The University of Chattanooga
Former Visiting Professor in Modern Languages
The Florida State University

EDITOR

Auguste Comte

TWAS 625

AUGUSTE COMTE

By ARLINE REILEIN STANDLEY

Indiana University–Purdue University
Fort Wayne

TWAYNE PUBLISHERS

A DIVISION OF G. K. HALL & CO., BOSTON

Published in 1981 by Twayne Publishers,
A Division of G. K. Hall & Co.
All Rights Reserved

Printed on permanent/durable acid-free paper and bound
in the United States of America

First Printing

Library of Congress Cataloging in Publication Data

Auguste Comte.

(Twayne's world authors series ; TWAS 625. France)
Bibliography: pp. 168–74
Includes index.
1. Comte, Auguste, 1798–1857.   I. Title.
II. Series.
B2248.S73   194   81-4107
ISBN 0-8057-6467-4   AACR2

To the memory of
Rosalie Colie
and her living art

Contents

About the Author

Arline Reilein Standley is on the faculty of Indiana University–Purdue University at Fort Wayne. She served as chairperson of the Department of English and Linguistics, Indiana University at Fort Wayne, from 1972–1975. She has also taught English as a foreign language in Belem and in Porto Alegre, Brazil, for four years.

Her academic work was done at the University of Iowa, where she served as research assistant to Professor Rosalie Colie and for *Philological Quarterly*. She received her Ph.D. in Comparative Literature from that university in 1967. She has received fellowships from the University of Iowa, Indiana University, and the National Endowment for the Humanities.

A long-time student of English, French, and Brazilian literature, Professor Standley is at present working on a comparative study dealing with the effects of regionalism on Brazilian and American fiction. Novelists to be included in this analysis are William Faulkner, John Steinbeck, José Lins do Rêgo, Graciliano Ramos, and Guimarães Rosa.

Preface

Where W. M. Simon begins his examination of *European Positivism in the Nineteenth Century* with Lewis Carroll's Humpty Dumpty reflecting on the delightful privilege of making a word mean just what you choose it to mean, the present study begins rather with the frustrated efforts of all the king's horses and all the king's men to put the sadly fractured Humpty Dumpty of nursery rhyme together again. The work of Comte has become similarly atomized; we find it mentioned in so many contexts and in such contradictory ways that it is difficult to sort out what Comte really said or what he was really significant for. This study is an attempt to fit together at least some of the larger pieces.

Our overview, then, is not directed to the Comte specialist, but to the person familiar enough with Comte's name to silently file it under Positivism, yet not very familiar with Comte's works, which are, we are told repeatedly, so excessively long and so tediously unrelieved with wit. Our aim is to outline the evolution of Comte's thought (wittily, of course), to explicate his major works (as briefly as may be), to explore his basic assumptions ("basic," since his works are shot through with assumptions), and to demonstrate some of the major ways in which Comte's ideas were influential (in the intellectual, religious, social-political, and aesthetic realms, no less). Such an ambition surely calls for all the king's horses, all the king's men, and a good deal of epoxy glue besides.

This kind of overview of Comte's thought is not now much in vogue, probably because in our time the need to specialize has become even more imperative than it was in his. Nevertheless, an important aspect of the Comtean canon is its encyclopedic nature— its ambition to synthesize all knowledge and to comprehend all human experience. Comte's sense of the intellectual, religious, and social fragmentation of his time brought forth his "positive" response to all of these problems seen as a whole. By *positive* he meant a response predicated on reality and usefulness, but also including certainty, precision, organicism, and relativism—all qualities generally associated with positive (that is, scientific) knowledge.

Comte's Positivism was to incorporate all these "highest attributes of human wisdom" and to add to them the union of moral with intellectual qualities. By systematizing feelings (through the Religion of Humanity) as he had earlier systematized thought (through his two general "laws" governing the intellect), Comte claimed that Positivism had synthesized the subjective and objective realms, and that it alone could restore intellectual, moral, and social unity. Comte's analysis and his Positive solution give us a broad perspective on the problems confronting the nineteenth century and the twentieth as well. Today the problem of disunity is greater still, for technological progress has given us more nightmarish possibilities. Though Comte was wrong about the duration of the crisis, his analysis of its nature was, as Eric Voegelin points out, often perceptive and relevant to our time. Perhaps we can learn, too, from his proposed solution and from its own nightmarish possibilities. At any rate, it is always helpful to define where we are by reference to where we have been. Comte's work can be useful in this effort, but it is most useful if we can see it whole.

The pieces that are put together in this book come from many sources. Basic material comes from Comte's own works and letters, from contemporaries' comments about him and his works. These "classic" sources include John Stuart Mill, Emile Littré, Dr. J. F. E. Robinet, Richard Congreve, George Henry Lewes, Herbert Spencer, George Eliot, and many others. Any investigator of Comte's life and work must also be particularly grateful for Henri Gouhier's research on Comte's life and formative years, and for W. M. Simon's exemplary study of Positivist influence in Europe. For explication and evaluation of Comte's ideas in particular fields, the experts in those areas have been a most valuable source of information. Those from whom we have pilfered most are Pierre Arnaud, Raymond S. Aron, André Cresson, Georges Dumas, Herbert Marcuse, F. S. Marvin, Eric Voegelin. A more complete list of sources is to be found in the bibliography. Needless to say, none of these sources is responsible for errors or for the sometimes eccentric interpretations that have made their way into this book.

ARLINE R. STANDLEY
Indiana University–Purdue University at Fort Wayne

Acknowledgments

I am grateful to Indiana University–Purdue University at Fort Wayne for its support of my research: a sabbatical leave enabled me to do substantial work on this project. Special thanks are due to Dean Dwight Henderson, whose Arts and Letters Division provided much-needed help in preparing the manuscript. In addition, the library staff also helped me immeasurably—particularly Ruth Harrod, who is unparalleled in getting books through inter-library loan. I wish also to thank others whose encouragement and assistance have made this book possible: my father and mother, George and Adeline Reilein, for their loyal support; Dr. Sylvia Bowman, for kindnesses innumerable; Dr. Hermine van Nuis, for sound counsel; Nancy Nielsen, Marci Irey, and especially Barbara Blauvelt, for help in preparing the manuscript. I am particularly grateful to Dr. Maxwell Smith for his careful editing, his thoughtful suggestions, and his unending patience.

The greatest debt of all is that which I owe to Rosalie Colie, mentor and friend. To her living memory I dedicate this book as a small payment on account.

Chronology

1798   January 19. Birth of Auguste Comte in Montpellier. (Christened Isidore-Auguste-Marie-François-Xavier Comte.)

1807–1814   Studied at the Lycée Impérial at Montpellier.

1814–1816   Studied at the École Polytechnique in Paris.

1816   April: provisional closing of the École Polytechnique by the Restoration government. Comte returned to Montpellier; wrote *Mes Reflections;* took courses in medicine and physiology at the city's Faculty of Medicine; went back to Paris and began to teach mathematics for a living.

1817   August: Comte's association with Saint-Simon began.

1818–1821   Collaboration with Saint-Simon on *Le Politique, L'Industrie, L'Organisateur, Du Système industriel, Catéchisme des industriels.*

1822   Publication of the "Prospectus des travaux scientifiques nécessaires pour réorganiser la Société" in *Système industriel.*

1824   May: broke with Saint-Simon over the publication of the "Prospectus."

1825   February: civil marriage of Auguste Comte and Caroline Massin. "Considérations philosophiques sur les sciences et les savants" and "Considérations sur le pouvoir spirituel" published in Saint-Simon's *Le Producteur.*

1826   April: Comte began teaching his course in Positive Philosophy at his home. Experienced a severe mental breakdown and was sent to the clinic of Dr. Esquirol for treatment. December: Comte dismissed from the clinic "uncured" and returned home. Religious marriage of Comte and Caroline Massin.

1827   April: Comte attempted suicide. By the end of this year he was again able to work.

1829   January: Comte resumed teaching his course in Positive Philosophy.

1830   Publication of Volume I of the *Cours de philosophie positive*. The succeeding volumes appeared in 1835, 1838, 1839, 1841, and 1842.

1831   Began his free course in popular astronomy for the general public. (Continued to teach this course until 1848.)

1832   Appointed Assistant Lecturer in Analysis and Mechanics at the École Polytechnique.

1836   Appointed Admissions Examiner at the École Polytechnique.

1837   Death of Comte's mother.

1841   Moved to No. 10, rue Monsieur-le-Prince. (This later became the headquarters of Positivism.) November: beginning of correspondence with John Stuart Mill.

1842   Final separation from his wife, Caroline.

1844   "Discours sur l'esprit positif," preamble to *Traité philosophique d'astronomie populaire*. Comte not reappointed as Examiner for the École Polytechnique. Mill (and later Littré) raised funds to make up Comte's loss of income. October: Comte met Clotilde de Vaux, sister of one of his former students.

1845   The "incomparable year" of Comte's love for Clotilde (who offered him only friendship).

1846   April 5: death of Clotilde.

1848   Founding of the Positivist Society. *Discours sur l'ensemble du positivisme*.

1849   Comte established the Universal Church of the Religion of Humanity. Positivist Calendar.

1851   Comte lost his position as Assistant Lecturer at the École Polytechnique. Publication of the first volume of the *Système de politique positive ou Traité de sociologie instituant la religion de l'humanité*. Subsequent volumes appeared in 1852, 1853, and 1854. Littré (and others) resigned from the Positivist Society when Comte supported the *coup d'état* of Louis Napoleon.

1852   *Catéchisme positiviste ou sommaire exposition de la religion universelle*. December: letter to Czar Nicholas I.

1855   *Appel aux conservateurs*. December: Comte wrote his will.

1856   *Synthèse subjective ou système universel des conceptions propres à l'état normal de l'humanité*. Comte proposed to the Jesuit Superior an alliance against Western anarchy.

1857   September 5: death of Comte. September 8: burial at Père-Lachaise.

CHAPTER 1

Comte, the Man and the Career

HENRI Gouhier begins his biography of Auguste Comte with Comte's own reflection on his life: *"Car c'est un roman que le fond de ma vie . . . et un fort roman qui paraîtrait bien extraordinaire, si jamais je le publiais sous des noms supposés."*[1] ("For the real part of my life is like a novel—a powerful novel which would seem very extraordinary, if ever I published it with fictional names.") When the young Comte wrote this (in November 1825), he had scarcely lived through the opening chapters of that "novel." As the years passed, the episodes became still more extraordinary—so strange, in fact, that they create for the biographer the problem of verisimilitude. At any rate, Gouhier piously uses these words to remind himself as biographer not to novelize a second time.[2]

To complicate matters even more, there are exceedingly different interpretations of Comte's life and work. Was Comte indeed the saintly and martyred High Priest of Humanity that his faithful disciple Dr. Robinet saw? Or was he the brilliant dreamer whom Emile Littré (a faithful Positivist, but not a faithful disciple) saw—the dreamer who became so possessed by his dream that he lost sight of his own fundamental intellectual (and moral?) principles?

Robinet, like the master himself, claimed that the whole of Comte's life was dedicated to a work which is a unity.[3] Littré, on the other hand, found the early and late phases of Comte's work irreconcilable.[4] For Littré, Comte's attempt to base a morality on science while subjecting science to morality seemed fatally contradictory in its duality. The particular difficulty that this duality creates for the biographer lies in the fact that Comte's life and work became more and more interwoven during the last fifteen years of his life. When the philosopher became the High Priest of the Religion of Humanity, his disciples had to make their choice. Eventually biographer and reader, too, must choose between these interpretations: was he a high priest of humanity or a lost dreamer? But this is to anticipate. Let us begin at the beginning.

I *Background*

Comte's family background could hardly have been more conventional. His father, Louis-Auguste Comte, was a humble employee of the tax office in the Department of Hérault. As a civil servant, his highest ambition was to become tax collector for the district of Montpellier. He was a family man and a solid citizen— regular in his habits and respected by his acquaintances. He married, in 1797, one Félicité-Rosalie-Boyer. The Catholic ceremony was a secret one because the revolutionary government had closed the churches of Montpellier, the centers of conservative political activities. Like her husband, Rosalie was a conservative, a term which in those times signified Royalist and Catholic. She seems, however, to have had a much more warmly sentimental nature than her husband. She wrote in a letter that she had too much warmth of heart, too strong a sensibility for her own peace. Rosalie devoted this fund of tender concern to her husband and then to her children, the two sons and two daughters that blessed their marriage. The first of these children made his appearance on January 20, 1798, and was given the name Isidore-Auguste-Marie-François-Xavier Comte. Long after this child had grown up, gone off to Paris, and decided to call himself Auguste, his mother continued to fuss over her "petit Isidore." The Comtes soon had a daughter, Hernance, who lived but a few months. Later there came a second son, Adolphe, and a daughter, Alix. In this family group Isidore grew up.

Not even the warmth of the mother, however, served to create a happy, closely knit family. Only Alix, who remained at home and cared for her parents in the illness and poverty of their old age, seems to have shown much regard for them. Adolphe, when grown, got into bad company and came to an early death in Martinique. Auguste, in Paris, at times wrote warmly, at times broke completely with his family.

II   *Education*

The Comtes managed, though their income was meager, to put the two boys through the Lycée at Montpellier. *Le Comtou*, as Isidore-Auguste was nicknamed because of his small size, entered the Lycée when he was nine years old. Under the Napoleonic regime the Lycées were boarding schools which served as the training grounds for future soldiers and civil servants of the Empire. The students wore drab uniforms, were divided into companies, and moved to the sound of drums under the direction of a drill master, who also taught the handling of arms. The better students received the ranks of sergeant major or corporal. Since such schools were not popular with the bourgeoisie, Gouhier accounts for Auguste's presence there by conjecturing that he may have received some kind of scholarship aid because his father was a civil servant.

Despite the dullness of the Lycée routine, Auguste began there to show remarkable skills. He won a copy of the *Iliad* as first prize for "éloquence française." He astonished everyone with his prodigious feats of memory: he could repeat hundreds of lines of verse after one hearing, for example, or recite backwards all the words on a page he had read but once. His precocity was such that, having finished but one year of the special mathematics course, he was ready to take the entrance examination for the École Polytechnique. Since he was only fifteen and therefore not yet eligible for admission to the École Polytechnique, Auguste remained at the Lycée one more year.

Other facets of Auguste's character began to manifest themselves in the activities of these school years. Too serious to take part in the normal schoolboy diversions, he was, nonetheless, involved in a number of rows. Though submissive to his intellectual superiors, he was in the vanguard of those who refused to recognize the arbitrary authority of inadequate teachers and rigid administrators. It was in these adolescent years that he rebelled, in the name of liberty, against all authority: that of the school, that of the faith, that of the government.

A different kind of experience, prophetic, perhaps, took place during Auguste's final year at the Lycée. His most-admired instructor, Daniel Encontre, asked him one day to substitute teach for him in the special mathematics class. It may have been that day that Auguste Comte found his vocation. At any rate, throughout his life

he was, above all else, a teacher. He taught when he examined
students for the École Polytechnique, when he talked with his
friends, when he wrote letters, when he penned the *Course of
Positive Philosophy* and *The System of Positive Policy*, and even
when he wrote his will and testament.

Comte, having passed the admission examination, enrolled at the
École Polytechnique on October 30, 1816. The new student described in the register was anything but prepossessing in appearance: "Hair and eyebrows chestnut blond, large forehead, snub
nose, reddish brown eyes, medium mouth, round chin, oval face,
height 1 meter 59 centimeters [about 5'2"], . . . smallpox marked,
scar on right ear."[5] He was, however, on the basis of his good
examination grades, admitted as a corporal in the student ranks.

The École Polytechnique was, Comte wrote to a friend, the best
school in the world. It had prospered under Napoleon once he
realized that it was his best source of military officers and engineers.
Like the Lycée, the school was organized after the model of the
military service. It is difficult to imagine a student of Comte's spirit
accepting with equanimity the strict regimentation. Despite the
deadening routines, Comte found himself so much at home that he
dreamt of never leaving the École. Traces of his rebellious spirit
still remained, however. He managed to get a reputation as a trou-
blemaker when a group of students broke the student curfew. Then,
in April 1816, he was one of six student representatives who demanded that geometry instructor M. Lefebvre change his way of
dealing with the students. When the director, General Dejean, tried
to punish the six ringleaders, he found the whole student body in
rebellion. The general, hoping to reassure the new conservative
government that the École Polytechnique was not a hotbed of re-
publicanism and revolution (not an easy task since it had actively
supported Bonaparte), proposed that fifteen of the student activists
be dismissed. The government responded by simply sending two
detachments of troops to close the school. The students were
shipped off to their homes without further incident.

Comte, with some of his friends, organized an Association of the
Students of the École Polytechnique, but his efforts accomplished
little except to signify to the government that the rebellion was not
over. The government responded with secret police surveillance
over Comte's activities. A meditation, written by Comte in June
1816 but unpublished until 1882, attests to unmistakably revolu-

tionary tendencies. Its title echoes the rallying cries of the revolution:

MY REFLECTIONS
Humanity, Truth, Justice, Liberty, Fatherland.
Comparisons [*rapprochements*] between the regime of
1793 and that of 1816
addressed to the French People.
COMTE
student of the ex-École Polytechnique (June 1816).

The police, however, turned up no evidence of conspiracy, and in July Comte received without difficulty a passport permitting him to return to Paris.

At this time Comte was elated over the prospect of a position as professor of mathematics in the United States. The government there was considering the establishment of a school like the École Polytechnique. Unfortunately, the American Congress, while supporting the idea of founding such a school, postponed indefinitely specific action on the project. Comte, who had thrown himself wholeheartedly into preparations for this adventure, was bitterly disappointed.

By mid-August 1816, the École Polytechnique had reopened. Comte talked of applying for readmission, and when he saw that other leaders of the April disturbance were permitted to reenter, he felt reassured that he would be allowed back. The deadline for him to apply for readmission came and went, however, without Comte's making the necessary application. Whatever his motive, Comte failed to move, and this decision cost him dearly. Lacking a degree, Comte was forever at a disadvantage in the teaching profession.

As Comte looked about for some means of support, friends helped him find private pupils to tutor and books to translate. Although such occupations may have left him freer than a regular teaching position would have, they provided at best a precarious livelihood. For a time Comte worked as private secretary to Casimir Périer. Then, in 1818, he became secretary to Claude Henri de Saint-Simon, thus beginning a working relationship which was to last for seven years. Although the nature and extent of Saint-Simon's influence on Comte are the subject of endless discussion, Comte himself

regarded this step as the beginning of a new era in his life. It was
at this point that he baptized himself anew, so to speak: he no longer
called himself Isidore, but Auguste.

III   *Personal and Professional Life*

While serving his apprenticeship with Saint-Simon, Comte
worked with him on many publications, most of which came out
under Saint-Simon's name. In the process, Comte came to share
many of his mentor's interests. But as his own thoughts took shape,
the role of cherished pupil became increasingly irksome to him.
Comte became critical of Saint-Simon's lack of scientific knowledge
and his unsystematic approach. The disagreement became an open
quarrel between them when Comte insisted upon his rights as the
author of the "Plan des travaux scientifiques." When it was finally
published in 1824, Comte felt himself betrayed, and from this point
on he regarded Saint-Simon as his Lucifer.[6]

Meanwhile, in 1821 Comte had first met Caroline Massin, a nine-
teen-year-old girl of the streets, who was to become, a few years
later, his wife. In the "Secret Addition" to his Testament Comte
tells the "fatal secret" of her life, by way of justifying his own shift
of affection from this "unworthy wife" to the "angelic" Clotilde de
Vaux.[7] Suffice it to say that the young Caroline had been raised by
a loose-living actress mother, who hoped to realize a good profit
from the girl's virginity. And so it was. Long before Comte met her,
the sixteen-year-old Caroline had been taken up by a young Paris
lawyer, M. Cerclet. Although it was a short liaison, according to the
"Secret Addition," M. Cerclet never really disappeared from her
life. About Cerclet, M. Gouhier says, not without a touch of malice,
"It is curious to note that he rarely shows up with empty hands."[8]
By 1819, however, Caroline was left on her own without a profession
or protector and was listed on the police register as a prostitute.

After their brief acquaintance in 1821, Caroline dropped from
Comte's view. Toward the end of 1822 he found her set up in a
bookshop, thanks to the renewed generosity of M. Cerclet. Caroline,
a bright young woman, began studying mathematics with Comte.
(M. Cerclet, too, became an algebra student.) By March 1824 Caroline and Comte were sharing an apartment, and before long she
persuaded him that marriage was a perfectly reasonable step.
Comte's parents naturally objected to such an imprudent match
even though they knew nothing of Caroline's background. They

pointed out that the young couple had no regular source of income, and, besides, they had been living together in sin in the eyes of the Church. Comte persisted, however, until their grudging consent was won. On February 19, 1825, a civil ceremony legalized their marriage. Among the witnesses was Antoine Cerclet. It was M. Cerclet, too, who apparently performed the singular service of seeing that the name of Caroline Massin was erased from the police register. No trace of her inscription on that *infame registre* remained.

The existence of the young couple was hand-to-mouth. Comte had one student and a number of debts. A small sum of money came mysteriously into Caroline's hands and relieved their poverty temporarily. Then Comte was asked to write for *Le Producteur* (a journal edited by one M. Cerclet), and he supplied the three articles entitled "Philosophic Considerations regarding the Sciences and Scholars." Financial difficulties were not the only problems the young couple faced. Marital tensions developed when Caroline did not prove to be as submissive as Comte thought proper in a wife.

The year 1826 was a period of crisis for Comte. In January he announced a scheme which he hoped would not only provide income, but also give him the opportunity to teach his new philosophy. He proposed to give a subscription series of seventy-two public lectures over the course of a year (March 1826 to March 1827). Plunging into his preparations in a fever of excitement, Comte worked almost twenty-four hours a day. His agitation and intensity brought on nervous symptoms: feverish activity, irrational attacks, violent rages. On several occasions Caroline fled from him in fear.

On April 2, 1826, Comte began his Course in Positive Philosophy. The opening session drew a distinguished audience, most of them scientists. After giving three lectures, Comte suffered a breakdown and was hospitalized for several months at the private clinic of M. Esquirol, a pioneer in the scientific analysis and treatment of madness. Comte's mother, rushing to Paris, began official action to have Comte committed to an asylum, but Caroline fought the suit.

On December 2, 1826, Comte, "uncured" after eight months of clinical treatment, was discharged and given into the care of his wife. He was still violent. For example, on the way home he rewarded with a sharp blow the friend who reminded him gently that they were riding through Paris, not Constantinople. At mealtime he would plunge a knife into the table, in the style of one of Scott's wild highlanders, and fling it at Caroline when the service was not

quick enough. He was still irrational, too. His mother, convinced
that his madness was the result of the sin of living with Caroline
without the blessing of the Church, had arranged for a priest to
perform the religious marriage on Comte's return home. While the
priest went through the ritual, Comte carried on an antitheological
harangue and then triumphantly signed the certificate: Brutus
Bonaparte Comte.

Robinet insists that it was Comte's mother who nursed him back
to health,[9] but it appears rather that it was Caroline who cared for
him ably and heroically. Smoothing away all opposition, she created,
for the time at least, the peaceful atmosphere he needed. She even
managed to get him to take quietly the prescribed medicines and
purges by taking them herself along with him. Within six weeks
Comte was over the crisis, although he remained acutely depressed
(in a state of quasi-vegetation, he himself said) throughout the following year. On one occasion (in April 1827) he threw himself into
the Seine in an attempt at suicide, but he was quickly rescued. It
was Caroline, whatever her faults, who restored him to health.
Furthermore, it was during the course of this unsatisfactory marriage, in the period from 1830 to 1842, that Comte wrote the work
for which he is best known, the *Cours de philosophie positive*.

Those twelve years were difficult ones. Comte's family and friends
helped out financially during the period of his illness, but for some
time there was no regular income. The domestic situation was not
improved by Caroline's offers (or threats?) to go back to her old
métier in order to supply bare necessities. Comte was unable to get
a regular appointment at the École Polytechnique, but was, in 1832,
given a minor post as lecturer *(répétiteur)* there. This employment
provided a small income. An additional appointment as entrance
examiner gave Comte for the first time (in 1837) a regular and
reasonably adequate income.

From time to time marital tensions became acute. Three times
Caroline left, only to return. (Twenty years later, in the "Secret
Addition," Comte gave as reasons for these breaks Caroline's need
for unrestrained liberty and her inability to dominate.) As Comte
worked on the final segment of the Positive Philosophy—his crowning vision of a new science, sociology—he was again in much the
same state as he had been early in 1826. His irritability led to a final
break with Caroline. It led also to a violent attack on the "establishment" of the École Polytechnique in a diatribe which he rashly
published in the Preface to Volume VI of the *Cours*. Himself fearing

another breakdown, Comte refused to let Caroline leave until the final volume of this work was published. A few days after the book came out (August 1, 1842), Caroline left him. The marriage was over.

The attack on the personnel of the École Polytechnique had its consequences, too. From that time on Comte's reappointment was uncertain. Indeed, in 1844 his lectureship was not renewed. To some extent Comte's "persecutions" did represent the resistance of the establishment to new ideas. Our sympathies are often with Comte in his refusal to compromise even when it would have served his self-interest. On the other hand, Comte was undoubtedly a difficult person to work with and brought many of his troubles upon himself. In the case of his teaching, for example, he arrogantly cut his lecture time, eliminated standard materials, and spoke ill of his colleagues. Although Comte seems to have been a capable teacher, it is hardly surprising that his attack convinced the École Polytechnique that it could get along without him.

When the blow fell, help came from across the Channel—from John Stuart Mill, who undertook with some of his friends to put together a fund sufficient to sustain Comte for a year. Unfortunately, when the subsidy ran out, Comte, who held that as a spiritual leader he had the right to such support, accused these men of abandoning him. Mill's reply was simply that neither he nor his friends regarded Comte as spiritual leader. While he disclaimed discipleship, Mill did try to renew the subsidy. He did not, however, succeed in getting together enough money to support Comte. Somewhat later Emile Littré, the French journalist, managed to set up a regular subscription fund for Comte. Eventually the support of the high priest of Positivism became part of Comte's system, but this preliminary attempt to establish public support for the spiritual leader failed.

Mill's acquaintance with Comte's work went back to the 1820s, the days of his interest in the Saint-Simonians. As the volumes of the *Cours* came out in the 1830s, Mill had read them and recommended them to many of his friends and fellow intellectuals. In 1841 Mill and Comte began a correspondence which continued for many years. While Mill was never really a disciple of Comte's, the famous Utilitarian lent prestige to Positivism by his favorable comments in his *System of Logic* (1843) and in private letters.[10] Even in 1865, long after Comte had publicly denounced Mill for his failure to commit himself to the Positive polity, Mill's essay "Auguste

Comte and Positivism," in the *Westminster Review*, dealt even-
handedly with the great contribution Comte had made to the
thought of the time. Despite Mill's reservations all along, he regarded Comte as one of the greatest thinkers of the time—com-
parable, he wrote in this article, to Descartes and Leibniz in their
generations. At the same time Mill regretted and warned against
the dangerous totalitarianism to which Comte's obsession with system had led him.[11]

Meanwhile, in France the publication of the six-volume *Cours*
(1830–1842) had elicited not one single article. At the end of 1844,
however, Emile Littré published six articles dealing with the Comtean philosophy.[12] This was a decisive moment, marking the beginning of a wider dissemination of Positivism in France. The writer
of the articles, Littré, was an eminent academician and a forthright,
intelligent journalist. He became one of Comte's supporters (both
intellectually and financially) and continued to call himself a disciple
of Positivism even after he and Comte had serious differences over
the Religion of Humanity, politics, and Comte's treatment of Caroline.

The crux, for Littré and for Mill, was Comte's grand project for
the reorganization of society, the *Système de politique positive*
("Positive Polity"), which Comte hoped to begin publishing in October 1844. Again, nervous excitement brought on illness. That
October he met Mme Clotilde de Vaux and fell passionately in love
with this young woman, who had been left to her own resources
when her husband was convicted of a felony. Comte, failing to make
her his mistress, made her instead his Beatrice, his holy saint. Their
relationship, an ecstatic one for Comte, at least, did not last long,
and Clotilde's death of tuberculosis on April 5, 1846, was an ultimate
test of his ability to resist a breakdown. Comte did not succumb,
but went on to create the Religion of Humanity and to complete
the projected four volumes of the *Système* (1851–1854). Comte's
"incomparable year" had its effect on the polity; for, even though
Comte had in his earliest publications stressed the spiritual foundations of the new society he envisioned, it was the motivating
power of love that finally transformed the "demonstrable religion"
of science into the Religion of Humanity. Interestingly enough, the
forms of the new religion were modeled on those of the Catholic
Church—the very Church the young Isidore had so violently rejected: the basic doctrines of the Religion of Humanity were spelled
out in the *Catéchisme;* its saints were commemorated in the Posi-

tivist Calendar; and its sacraments, like those of Catholicism, ritualized the decisive moments in man's passage through life.

In the political struggle of 1848–1851 Comte's political views, too, seemed to take a giant step backward. Despite his sympathy for the proletariat, he thought that the people were "seduced by the utopias of the Reds."[13] Consequently, when the moment of choice came in the *coup d'état* of December 1851, Comte backed Louis Napoleon Bonaparte. Anything was better than anarchy or the tyranny of the Reds. This decision set off a heated argument in the Positivist Society and led to the resignation of a number of members, among whom the foremost was M. Littré. Nonetheless, Comte defended his choice and later (in 1855) issued an "Appeal to the Conservatives" proposing a union—a religious league—between the Catholics and the Positivists to combat the Communists and the Liberals. The man who had sought to create a system accommodating both order and progress seemed to have opted, finally, for order.

Comte became more and more isolated from the world. He had for many years practiced what he called *hygiène cérébrale*—that is, he refused to clutter his mind by reading the multitude of books being published. Needless to say, this "mental hygiene" left him out of touch with the scientific and other developments of his day, and it accounts for some of the mistakes and bizarre elements in his work.[14]

The pattern of Comte's daily life took on the aspect of a monastic regimen in its rigorously observed hours and Spartan diet. His day began at 5 A.M and ended at 10 P.M. The mornings and afternoons were given over to the constant work of "meditation, study and editing." He was preoccupied with the ritual prayers and commemoration of Clotilde, the inspirer of the new religion and representative of the great Being, Humanity. In his reading Comte now turned to the great poets. His daily devotions included one chapter of the *Imitation of Christ* and one canto of the *Divine Comedy*. Indeed, Comte seems to have moved in spirit into Dante's empyrean heights with Clotilde playing alternately the roles of Beatrice and the Virgin Mary. Although he still worked on treatises dealing with the familiar subjects of mathematics, education, and industry, Comte's approach had changed, as even the title of his new work indicates: *Synthèse subjective*. The scientific prevision aimed at in his earlier works gave way to an almost poetic vision. The point of view changed: he proposed to treat his subject under the supposition that he was writing in 1927. The structure of the work became

Dantean—governed by an elaborate set of rules which Comte observed throughout the 800 pages. In this work, form and language themselves were to be made to reflect as well as express the structure of the whole synthesis.

But even this exercise of discipline did not occupy his mind completely. As ever, Comte's mind projected into the future with a schedule of the works he still had to produce. He would complete the *Synthèse*, parts II and III. The dates for projected works were laid out as part of Comte's grand plan. In 1858 would appear the first volume of the *Système de morale positive*, to be dedicated to his mother. This would be the first volume of his long-promised treatise on universal education. The next year, 1859, the second volume, adding "practical morality" to the "theoretic," would be forthcoming. The *Système de l'industrie positive*, promised since 1822, would see publication in 1861. In 1862, the Jesuits would be addressed in an *Appel aux Ignatius*, which would propose a "spiritual league" between the Positivists and Jesuits: "The two clergies could, in the name of reason and morality, oblige all those who believe in God to become Catholics and all those who do not believe in Him to become Positivists, eliminating by mutual agreement [*d'un commun accord*] Protestantism, Deism, and Skepticism, which are the three stages of the modern sickness."[15] The year 1864, the twentieth anniversary of the meeting of Comte and Clotilde, would be marked by the publication of the "sacred correspondence" between the two, as well as other biographical materials concerning them. In addition, Comte proposed the publication of the daily prayers, the annual confessions, and his own testament (written in 1855). As a special commemoration, he planned to give an outline of a poem in thirteen cantos on his "second life." In 1867, in honor of his seventieth birthday, Comte promised a treatise on *La Philosophie première*.

Though all of these remained mere projections in Comte's immensely fertile mind, he had in actuality continued over the years his educational plans for the working class. In addition to the free courses he had given at the Mairie and at the Palais Cardinal, he had designed a "great books" reading list specifically for the education of Positivists.

Comte passed his last years with Sophie Bliaux and her family. Sophie was not only a disciple, but an "adopted daughter" to him. She became, with the now-idealized Rosalie and with the ever-adored Clotilde, one of the saintly models of womanhood. Each represented a particular aspect of the high calling of woman—as daughter, as mother, and as wife.

Surrounded by a small group of disciples, Comte took all too seriously his duties as the director of their consciences. There were the weekly services on Wednesday evenings, and, in addition, Comte also made himself available to anyone for discussion and counseling all other evenings from seven to nine. His insistence on total submission was hardly more successful with the disciples than it had been with Caroline. The penalty for independence was recrimination and excommunication, as disciples like Littré and Blignière (an army officer) found out. Among the faithful were people from all walks of life. There were a number of doctors: J. F. E. Robinet, Foley, Georges Audiffrent, and L. A. Ségond. The favorite disciple was Pierre Lafitte, who after Comte's death became head of the Positivist Committee, though not the High Priest of the Religion of Humanity. The group also included Fabien Magnin (a carpenter), Fili (a mechanic), Charles Yundzill (a poet), Joseph Lonchampt (a polytechnician), and Hippolyte Déroisin (the future mayor of Versailles). In addition to this central group there were Positivist missions requiring Comte's supervision—bands of devoted Positivists in Holland, Spain, England, and the United States. Comte always tended to exaggerate the size and importance of these groups. In reality, the Republic of the West was but a vision.

However difficult it was for Comte to deal with real human beings, he dedicated himself fully to the service of humanity. The Positivist motto, Order and Progress, had become absorbed into the Religion of Humanity, wherein Love was the principle, Order the foundation, and Progress the end. Comte's personal commitment to this ideal was symbolized in the dry crust of bread which served as dessert for his evening meal and which reminded him, each day as he chewed on it, of the hungry poor of this world.

On September 5, 1857, Death wrote Finis to this "novel." Comte had become ill in May after attending the funeral of an old friend, M. Vieillard. Throughout the summer there were alternating periods of illness and seeming convalescence. Robinet watched with increasing concern as each acute attack of vomiting and hemorrhage weakened Comte. Despite the pain and weakness occasioned by his long illness, Comte's end was peaceful. It was for him a reunion with his beloved Clotilde. It was for him the putting on of immortality—not in some Christian heaven, but in absorption into the oneness of Humanity, the Great Being whose existence is eternal.

Even from the world beyond Comte spoke to his friends through the testament which he had written toward the end of 1855. The most immediate provisions of the will dealt with Comte's precise instructions regarding his death and burial: no Catholic rites (before or after his death), no autopsy, no embalmment. He was to be laid out on his bed and not buried till unmistakably dead. He designated his burial place, the composition and route of the burial procession. He specifically excluded from participation in these last rites false disciples, representatives of his widow, and representatives of the École Polytechnique.

Although Comte was far from rich in worldly goods, he made a number of legacies. There were token bequests: the bust of Auguste was to go to his father; the lithograph portrait of himself was to go to his sister, Mlle Alix; the cherished portrait of Clotilde was for Sophie; certain books were designated for close disciples. The rest of his effects were to go to his successor as High Priest. He specified also that his home be maintained by the Positivist Society as the center of the Religion of Humanity.

The most controversial part of his will dealt with the annual pension of 2,000 francs that his executors were asked to continue to give Comte's widow. Both Comte and his executors regarded this as a generous enough gesture to keep Mme Comte from asserting her property rights. But Comte persisted in stressing even in this document her unworthiness as a wife, and described this obligation to her as "the result of the one truly serious fault" of his life. Mme Comte took the high line that such an insult made the pension impossible to accept. To the consternation of the executors, she then entered Comte's house, which she had left in 1842, and began to dispose of her property. The hostility between the widow and the Positivists grew increasingly acrimonious. The executors' ace was the Secret Addition to Comte's will in which Caroline's disgraceful past was made public. Littré backed Mme Comte in her contesting of Comte's will, and this dispute widened the breach between the two groups of Positivists. It was already apparent that the philosophy designed to bring unity to all mankind had done little to create harmony even within this small group.

IV Influences

"What is a great life? 'A thought of one's youth realized in maturity,' " wrote the poet Alfred de Vigny. Comte appropriated these words to characterize his own career. It is an apt description, for Comte's fundamental ideas were conceived early in life and developed with extraordinary concentration throughout the remainder of it. Clearly a life was, for him, not just a series of events or relationships, but that which the mind creates.

The influences on Comte's developing mind were diverse. He early left behind him the Catholic and Royalist beliefs of his parents, and yet the imprint of the early teachings remained, only to surface again in Comte's late teachings, religious and political. At the Lycée and later at the École Polytechnique Comte encountered teachers formed in the school of eighteenth-century revolutionary ideas. They were oriented to science, impatient with theology. Himself rebellious against any authority save intellectual or moral superiority, Comte absorbed their revolutionary ideas regarding government and their free-thinking religion.

While eighteenth-century themes formed the matrix in which Comte's thought developed, questions regarding those ideas had become more and more insistent by the time he came to maturity in the early nineteenth century. The revolution had not brought about a stable society. Furthermore, it had not succeeded in alleviating the sufferings of the poor either through increasing productivity or through more equitable distribution of the world's goods. Where, then, did the remedy for society's ills lie? Cannot a civilization throw off the restrictive bonds of inherited traditions and institutions so that it can progress? Can it not do this without destroying itself? Is the pattern of a society one of growth and of inevitable decay? Is religion an essential part of human nature and human society? Is it possible to deal scientifically with moral and social problems? How can the claims to individual liberty be reconciled with the need for a stable and unified society?

The revolutionary doctrines of Liberty, Equality, and Fraternity had obviously not provided answers to these questions. Despite the success of the Revolution itself, there was no agreement as to what kind of authority was to replace that of the destroyed monarchy (and church). The Republic which had replaced the Monarchy had given way to the Directory (1795–1799), and it, in turn, to the Consulate (1799–1804). Throughout this period and through the first half of the nineteenth century, there were all kinds of civil disorders ranging from riot to revolution. Periodically these disorders led to radical shifts of power. During Comte's early years Napoleon dominated the political scene. In 1804 the Consulate was replaced by the First

Empire under Napoleon. The defeat of Napoleon in 1814 brought about restoration of the Bourbon monarchy under Louis XVIII. This rule was interrupted by the return of Napoleon in 1815, but was restored again after the final defeat of Napoleon. The Revolution of 1830 established the July Monarchy of Louis Phillip. Another revolution in 1848 gave France its Second Republic under the presidency of Louis Napoleon Bonaparte. A *coup d'état* in December 1851 made Louis Napoleon dictator. The following year, Louis Napoleon became Emperor and the Second Empire was established. Behind these major power struggles were complex social, economic, and political issues. It is no wonder that, given this record, many intellectuals of the time, Comte among them, found the disorder of the nation the most compelling of problems.

Comte's chosen discipline, mathematics, and his scientific study at the École Polytechnique would seem to offer little to prepare him to broach such grand philosophical and social topics. But Comte's own interests were far from narrow. His reading in his youth, before he began his practice of "mental hygiene," was wide and intensive. He was particularly interested in history—not only that of the developing sciences, but the long sweep of civilization itself. Like others of his time, Comte was puzzled by the disparity between the sure progress of science and the inconclusive seesawing of conflicting social and economic theories. Like others whose training was in the sciences, Comte had a vision of a new world created by the scientists. The first step in this creation seemed logically to be the application of scientific method to social, political, and economic data. The rigorous training of the scientists, he felt, enabled them to observe accurately, to solve problems logically, and to test out hypotheses empirically. If scientists could only turn their microscopes and telescopes on human affairs, they might provide the leadership so desperately needed.

Comte saw this trend as having begun (for modern times, at least) in the work of Montesquieu and Vico. Comte discussed Vico's work very little, but he did credit him with "a profound sense of the existence of Sociological laws"—the "laws" being, of course, Vico's theory that all civilizations go through inevitable cycles of development. [16] Vico was important enough to Comte to appear on the Positivist Calendar in the illustrious company of Positivist Saints. Comte praised Montesquieu, too, for beginning to apply "scientific method to political phenomena." Comte saw the *Spirit of the Laws* as a preliminary attempt to collect and classify data for the purpose of arriving at generalizations about these facts. Comte felt, however, that Montesquieu had not been thorough enough in his analysis, and that he had gotten sidetracked in various ways from his main inquiry.[17] While neither Vico nor Montesquieu succeeded in creating a sociological or political science, each had taken, to Comte's mind, a significant step in that direction.

Somewhat closer to Comte's own time were three other intellectuals from whom Comte absorbed certain ideas. These three were Turgot, Condorcet, and Burdin. The first of these, the economist Turgot, had in his youth written a dissertation "On the Historical Progress of the Human Mind."[18] In this essay we find in seminal form a number of the ideas which Comte later elaborated in his own philosophical system. As Turgot began grappling with the whole of human knowledge, he set about organizing it so as to show its unity and connection. His purpose was to study this ensemble scientifically and to determine thereby whether or not one could perceive a general direction within each part and within the whole. This enterprise led him to the concept of a hierarchy of sciences—a progressive chain from physics to chemistry to biology. The developmental pattern which he discerned was that of progress through three stages. Comte later labeled these, in his "Law of the Three States," the Theological, the Metaphysical, and the Positive states. According to Turgot, the ancient theological conceptions were man's first attempts to explain phenomena. Taking as a model the self's own power of acting, primitive man assumed that gods (and later, a God) within were the cause of all movement. As knowledge increased, philosophers came to regard these theological explanations as absurd. They themselves explained things by using abstract concepts, such as essences and faculties. Only later did knowledge become scientific (i.e., "positive"), when scientists, observing the mechanical action of one substance or entity on another, began to form hypotheses that mathematics could develop and verify. Where Turgot had set forth this sketch of the development of knowledge as an idea on which to meditate, Comte was later to regard progress through these three stages as a fundamental sociological law.

For both men this theory involved the acceptance of relativism. The advent of science meant the renouncing of the old absolutist views, and the abandoning of the old inquiries into the "essence" of things, or into their "first" or "final causes." The scientist was to be content to observe phenomena as they are and to search for the patterns called "general laws." Applied to social history, this ap-

proach entailed a new view of the civilizations of the past. It enabled
Turgot and Comte to appreciate the accomplishments of the Middle
Ages, for example: they could no longer simply write that period
off as barbaric, or as colorfully "Gothic"; they no longer saw it, as
many of their contemporaries did, as a period of darkness when the
"light" of classical antiquity had, alas, faded from the earth. Although
medieval culture might seem retrograde to eighteenth- or nineteenth-century eyes, Turgot and Comte held that the contributions
that medieval leaders made to civilization were to be seen in the
context of their times. The social scientists' task was to analyze the
relationships—of one institution to another, of one culture to another, of one period to its own past and future. The old judgments
were as pointless as the condemnation of biology would be on the
grounds that it had not attained the elegant clarity of mathematics.

The mathematician Condorcet, too, expounded certain ideas
which influenced Comte in his development of social science. Condorcet's main interest was to create a social science based on mathematics. Though he was (like Hume) skeptical about the possibility
of attaining certainty in any area of human knowledge, he explored
the calculus of probabilities and its application "to the political and
moral sciences." Condorcet claimed that through the use of this
calculus "there are sure means of arriving at a very great probability
in some cases and of evaluating the degree of that probability in a
great number."[19]

Although K. M. Baker in his recent book, *Condorcet,*[20] stresses
the centrality of this "social mathematics" to all of Condorcet's works,
including the *Esquisse d'un tableau historique des progrès de l'esprit
humain,* this particular work has traditionally been interpreted much
as Comte read it. He regarded it as a theory about the progress of the
human mind which, like Turgot's, was a forerunner of his own work.
Comte dismissed Condorcet's "social mathematics" as a tool of social
science which might be useful in the future—but only after a long
period of collecting and classifying data. To Comte, the really important contribution of Condorcet to social science was his basic
theory, elaborated in the *Esquisse,* that man, in progressing from
barbarism toward perfection, has passed through nine stages. Each
stage was concluded and the next introduced by some significant
discovery (the alphabet or the art of printing, for example) or by some
great event (the Crusades, for example, or the French Revolution).
Eventually, Condorcet postulated, civilization will move into a tenth
epoch: an age in which inequities between nations and between

classes will come to an end; a future in which human nature will perfect itself physically, intellectually, and morally. Condorcet did not represent this perfection as an absolute end, to be once and for all time attained, but as an ongoing process in which education would play an important part. Comte regarded this historical sketch as Condorcet's major contribution to social science, even though he did not accept Condorcet's rather arbitrary way of marking off the epochs. Comte liked to picture himself as following directly in the line of the great eighteenth-century Encyclopedists, particularly Condorcet and Diderot. He shared their interest in science. Their efforts toward the systematization of knowledge seemed to him to represent a first step in coordinating knowledge. He also shared their faith that eventually science would be able to deal with moral and social phenomena.

Dr. Burdin, whose ideas are recorded in conversations set down by Saint-Simon in his *Mémoire sur la science de l'homme*, is far less important in the history of ideas than are Vico, Montesquieu, Turgot, and Condorcet. Nonetheless, the direction of his thought is reflected in the work of Comte. Burdin pointed out how all sciences had their beginnings in conjecture and were drawn (or called) by the "great order of things" to become positive (or scientific) in nature. He felt that for too long mathematics had been dominating science and that it was now time to challenge that rule. His own particular interest was the possibility of applying scientific method to physiology. This branch of study could become a science when it became based in its entirety on observed facts, for, he added, "there exists no phenomenon which could not be observed from the point of view of the 'physics' of simple substance, or from that of the 'physics' of organized bodies, which is physiology."[21] Burdin had thus begun to put together the next link in the chain of the sciences and to stress the empirical method of observation. He also foresaw that the hold of mathematics on science would not easily be loosened. Comte saw the development of this science of man (physiology) as a necessary step before the science of social and political man could emerge.

Other men, too, were searching for an adequate base for the reconstruction of society. Some, like Joseph de Maistre,[22] turned back to the past. To others, Babeuf[23] and Fourier,[24] for example, the rigidly planned community seemed the answer. Still others, looking at the impressive development of science and industry, saw there the promise of solid and forward-looking leadership for society as a whole. The socialism advocated by Saint-Simon, for example, was based on the utilization of the talents of industry's experts. These efficient leaders, he held, could organize production, making use of the latest scientific discoveries, and, in so doing, they would direct one of the state's most important functions—which is to provide productive work for all.

V *Apprenticeship*

Comte's Positivism developed naturally, then, gleaning ideas from many sources, but most immediately from Saint-Simon, with whom he was associated from 1817–1824. In 1817 the young Comte became secretary to Claude Henri de Rouvroy, Count of Saint-Simon (1760–1825). The boy was dazzled ("seduced," he said, looking back on the occasion)[25] by this famous revolutionary who had fought with Lafayette and Washington in the cause of liberty. Although Saint-Simon was close to sixty when Comte met him, he was a man to impress any one with his enormous energy and youthful enthusiasm. He was a nobleman who used his title or played the humble republican as it suited him. He was delighted with his new "pupil" (*élève*), as he called him, and soon Comte became a favored student and collaborator.

Saint-Simon was at that time busy publishing his work on *L'Industrie,* and he put his new secretary to work on volume three. Saint-Simon regarded this project as a continuation of the work of Bayle and the Encyclopedists: Part I was to show that the edifice constructed by the clergy—including the idea of God, the explanation of nature, the morality, and the social and political institutions—had been demolished by the critical ideas of the Enlightenment; Part II was to construct a system of "positive ideas" (a philosophy without God, the true science of nature, a this-world morality, a liberal politics). These were to be coordinated in a new *Encyclopedia of Positive Ideas*. Comte finished his task, and the work was published in October 1817. The result was disaster, for the Industriels, who had backed Saint-Simon in this project, found the ideas far too radical and withdrew their support. Despite a retraction by Saint-Simon, *L'Industrie* could not survive. Saint-Simon's response was to announce a new publication, *Le Politique* (incorporated in the names of himself, Comte, and La Chevardière). Soon after this (in 1819) he brought out another publication, *L'Organisateur,* this one incorporated in the names of himself and Comte. Again trouble—

the first issue was seized by the printer. Saint-Simon was put on trial this time, but emerged triumphant.

One of Saint-Simon's ideas was that a return to social stability could be effected only by substituting industrial and scientific leaders for the older (and outmoded) feudal and religious chiefs. A society so governed could be organized, he felt, for the production necessary to alleviate the sufferings of the poor. His concern for the poor became, finally, a new religion.

In his series of "Letters," "Considerations of the Measures to Be Taken . . . " (later collected in *Du Système industriel*), Saint-Simon proposed a "new Christianity," an idea which was fully developed in *Nouveau Christianisme* (1825). Saint-Simon based his new theology on belief in God. Developing the social implications of Christianity, Saint-Simon concluded that the whole aim of society ought to be "the amelioration of the moral and physical existence of the poorest class." The socialism which he advocated proposed, in essence, the reorganization of society to this end.

These projects represent some of Saint-Simon's attempts to publicize liberal ideas, to put himself into the limelight as a new leader, and to recoup his fortune. The last of these motives was not the least, for by this time his funds were depleted. He had given lavishly of time and money to liberal causes, and yet he had, of course, to live as befitted a count. In March 1823 despair overcame him and he "staged" a suicide attempt. By December, however, he had enthusiastically taken up a new project, the *Catéchisme des industriels*. By this time, Comte, the favored pupil, had become increasingly irritated with his master. The inevitable confrontation came with the publication of the *Catéchisme* in 1824.

Comte in looking back on his collaboration with Saint-Simon remembered it as a period of "unhappiness without compensation." It was not the only time that Comte's memories, distorted by bitterness, were to play him false. Evidence from his own letters and from the testimony of his friends shows that the relationship was, for a long time, a congenial one and that the apprenticeship was a valuable one for Comte. He absorbed many of Saint-Simon's interests and ideas. Among these were Saint-Simon's belief in the industrial character of modern society, the future of science, the need for a spiritual power, the need for the unity of all Europe, and the idea that politics would become a science of observation. But Saint-Simon had neither training in science nor the discipline to order his ideas systematically. He was, above all, an activist. His basic concept, that a kind of "universal gravitation" was the principle which would serve as a base for the new order, meant a return to a priori method. Thus his political proposals, far from being soundly based on a science of observation, were simply plans for tinkering with institutions. Although Saint-Simon eventually gave up the naive search for a comprehensive law of "universal gravitation," he never managed to put together a well-grounded philosophy. Hence his attempts at reorganization were disorganized and ineffective. To a mind as given to system as Comte's was, such lack of order was dismaying, to say the least. Like other Socialist schemes, that of Saint-Simon lacked the firm philosophic rationale which was, for Comte, a prerequisite for the restructuring of society.

The intellectual friction between Comte and Saint-Simon had a second major cause: Saint-Simon's misunderstanding of science. He did not understand scientific method, really. Nor did he grasp the importance of chemistry and botany and their relationship to the other sciences. This again was a fatal defect to one like Comte, whose whole philosophy was based, eventually, on the importance of all the sciences and their interrelatedness.

In addition to these differences of mind, there was Saint-Simon's complacent habit of presenting the work of Comte as that of a cherished pupil. Although at first Comte was no doubt proud of such patronage, it became more and more irritating. He came to feel that Saint-Simon was exploiting him. By the time Comte had written the "Prospectus des travaux scientifiques nécessaires pour reórganiser la société" (1822), his own basic philosophy was taking shape, and he saw himself no longer as pupil, but as the intellectual superior. The confrontation came. It was the proposed *Catéchisme des industriels* which brought it about. When Comte learned that Saint-Simon was going to publish his "Prospectus de travaux scientifiques . . ." under the title of the *Catéchisme* (a title wholly unrelated to its subject matter), without the author's name and with an introduction by Saint-Simon, Comte's accumulated wrath exploded. Although Comte carried his point, Saint-Simon delayed publication until 1824. When the work finally came out, it did carry Comte's own introduction. In it Comte, apparently trying to avoid a complete break, politely called himself Saint-Simon's *élève*. But Saint-Simon had also included his own preface. Upon reading this preface, which spoke patronizingly of the incompleteness and the sketchiness of the work, and which carefully pointed out essential differences between the mentor's ideas and those of *"notre élève,"* Comte felt himself betrayed.[26] From then on, the relationship between the two became more and more strained. Before long the break was complete. The pattern—intimacy, break, bitter recrimination—is one that Comte repeated again and again.

Despite the bitterness with which Comte looked back on this relationship, it was a fruitful one for him. Catching him up in the whirlwind of Saint-Simon's activities, it busied Comte with ideas for the reorganization of society and gave his own ideas a context in which to develop. Not the least of the advantages to Comte was the opportunity it provided him, young and unknown, to get his writings into print. It was perhaps from this early experience that Comte developed the habit of writing to an immediate audience—that is, his regular procedure became that of writing volume by volume, and only when specific plans for publication had been made. The association with Saint-Simon had also plunged Comte into a brilliant, exciting Parisian milieu. But the young provincial, however dazzled, was hardly one to remain forever the humble apprentice. It was time to move on.

CHAPTER 2

The Enterprise

I *The Diagnosis*

WHILE Comte had missed the excitement and trauma of the Revolution itself, he grew up in the confusion of its aftermath when indeed it must have seemed that all coherence was gone. The turbulence of the Revolution and Directoire was followed by that of Consulat and Empire, and then the defeat of Napoleon left everything open to question again. Under such circumstances, it is hardly surprising that an intellectual born in France in 1798 should decide that the need to establish social order was humanity's most pressing problem. "Answers" to the anarchy were not only divergent, but in total opposition. The two extreme positions are represented, on the one hand, by what Comte called the "Retrograde" party with its desire to return to old Feudo-Catholic absolutism and, on the other, by the "Critical Philosophy," with its advocacy of the Sovereignty of the People. Against the backdrop of such divergency, Comte set himself to analyze not only the present state of his society, but the reasons for these widely differing responses to it.

A number of essays written between 1819 and 1826 reflect Comte's early thinking on these subjects. Many years later, in 1854, he himself chose to reissue six of these essays as an Appendix to the fourth volume of the *Système de politique positive*. The reprinting of these youthful essays was Comte's way of demonstrating "the perfect harmony which exists between my youthful efforts and my matured conceptions" (IV, Gen. Appendix, i).[1] The continuity of his work had been obscured, he felt, by the magnitude of the task he had undertaken. A brief examination of these works should help us, then, to understand the work of Comte as an ensemble.

In his essay of July 1819 on "The Separation of Opinions from 'Aspirations' " Comte set forth some of his basic assumptions regarding politics. Borrowing Turgot's terminology, Comte posited the theory that politics were still in a "theological state" (IV, 498). Only as politics became a science, Comte held, could agreement on the complex social and political questions be reached. Comte also began, in this essay, to differentiate between the functions of various segments of the body politic. Carrying over from industry into politics the idea of the division of labor, Comte divided the body politic into three parts: the public, the "scientific politicians," and the rulers. Each segment should have its proper functions— functions which should be kept separate. The role of the public, for example, was to indicate its aspirations—to establish society's general goals. Once this was done, it would be the task of the (political) scientists to determine the measures necessary for effecting these ends. And finally, the responsibility for carrying out these measures would fall on the rulers.

Sketchy as Comte's ideas are in this two-page essay, they represent his diagnosis of the basic problem. On the theoretical side, social-political knowledge had to be brought up to date through scientific analysis. On the "practical" side, the social-political setup had to be reorganized to make use of this new "positive" knowledge and to make the functioning of the new body politic most efficient. As Comte refined and developed these ideas, they expanded to an all-encompassing philosophy of human history in which theory and practice are intertwined.

In the second of his essays, "A Brief Estimate of Modern History" (April 1820), Comte discussed the conditions of his time in the context of history. To explain present conditions Comte went back to medieval times—to the centuries when the Feudo-Catholic system attained its greatest splendor. During that period, extending from the eleventh to the sixteenth century, the seeds of the new society were introduced in two developments, one political and one intellectual: the freeing of the common man from serfdom and the introduction of science.

The developing sciences, in particular, emphasized a new kind of knowledge based on observed facts; and, along with this, they encouraged the right of free inquiry. From these two root ideas there came eventually such varied events as the Reformation, Copernican-Galilean astronomy, printing, "technology" (the development of the useful arts), the voyages of discovery. This very progress constituted a series of attacks on the blind faith and absolutism implicit in the old system. The attacks, intensifying in the sixteenth

and seventeenth centuries, culminated in the eighteenth century
with the breaking of both the Spiritual Power (Catholicism) and the
Temporal Power (Feudalism). This challenging of the ancient, outmoded Feudo-Catholic system by the combined forces of science
and industry revealed the double movement, constructive and destructive, which Comte described as the Revolution's distinguishing
characteristic. Comte saw his own time as a period in which two
coexisting systems were caught in conflict. The remnants of the old,
crumbling organization were mounting a last desperate effort to
resist the new.

> Thus the actual condition of society presents the coexistence of a declining
> and of an adult system. . . .
> The new system then needs to mount but one step more in order to
> reach a complete organisation and entirely to replace the ancient system.
> It only remains for it to complete its temporal and spiritual achievements;
> in temporal matters by gaining possession of the House of Commons, in
> spiritual by establishing Morals on principles solely deduced from obser-
> vation. In truth all is ready for this step; the means exist, we only require
> to use them. (IV, 526)

This essay shows Comte's views regarding science, as well as his
interest in historical process. Comte's close identification of science
with progress meant that he was inclined to rate progress in terms
of intellectual development, or, at least, to use science as a measuring stick of progress. The essay reveals, too, Comte's belief that
the conflict between the scientific-industrial system and the Cath-
olic-Feudal order was part of an inevitable developmental process.
There was, he implied, a determinable line of progress, and this
assumption lay behind his search for the "laws" of this movement.
The inevitability of the process suggests determinism, and Comte
eventually had to deal with this problem. In these two essays, however, Comte confined his analysis to a general statement regarding
the ills of his time and their historical roots, though he did insist
on the need for spiritual renovation based on scientifically (empirically) derived moral principles.

II *The Prospectus*

The third essay in this group, "Plan of the Scientific Operations
Necessary for Reorganizing Society," was written in May 1822. In
it Comte began to develop more specifically the ideas propounded

in the earlier essays. On this occasion he began to explain with more care his premises and his methodology. He also took this opportunity to announce the works he projected for the future.

This third essay contains, as Comte explained, "the fundamental discovery of Sociological Laws," decisively indicating his "philo-sophic and social tendencies" (IV, Gen. Appendix, iii). This article opens with Comte's analysis of the moral and political anarchy re-sulting from the dissolution of the ancient system. He claimed that society had not yet effected the necessary reorganization because both rulers and people failed to comprehend the general principles which alone (in his view) could provide a sound basis for a new structure. The rulers, attempting to reinstate the feudal-theological system as the only means of ending anarchy, failed to understand that the only way to return to that regime would be through the annihilation of science and the reinstatement of slavery. The people, for their part, had tried to base their new society on "negative" or "critical" doctrines. The dogma of unlimited liberty of conscience, for example, was one such doctrine. This "liberty" seemed to Comte simply an antitheological principle, not a constructive one. Such "weapons of war" were useful in the destruction of the old system, but could not, wrote Comte, be "metamorphosed into instruments of construction" (IV, 532). He viewed the whole emphasis on liberty and individualism as a hindrance to the establishment of a uniform system of ideas. "In astronomy, physics, chemistry, and physiology there is no such thing as liberty of conscience . . ." (IV, 531). The need, then, was to find an organic, constructive doctrine, that is, to discover the principles of social or political science.

Only the scientists, Comte claimed, represented a disinterested class with the capacity and intellectual training to elevate politics to the rank of science. And only a scientific base could provide the kind of "authority" which would make the new system respected by all.

The new science of society had, in Comte's view, to be related to all of the other sciences. It not only built on them, but followed a similar pattern of development. This process Comte generalized in his "Law of the Three States" (or stages), sketched in this early essay and elaborated most fully in his *Cours*. His theory began with the idea that each branch of knowledge "is necessarily obliged to pass through three theoretical states: the Theological or fictitious state; the Metaphysical or abstract state; lastly the Scientific or pos-itive state" (IV, 547). Furthermore, this "law" included the idea of a hierarchy, in that Astronomy, Physics, Chemistry, and Physiology, in orderly sequence, have become positive, or scientific. Understandably then, politics could only become a science after all the other branches of knowledge preceding it in the hierarchy had become positive. Comte held that the science of society had passed through the first two of these stages and was now ready to enter the third.

His project included three series of works: the systematization of historical observations regarding the general progress of the human intellect as the basis for a Positive polity; a complete system of Positive education; and a "general exposition of the Collective Action which civilised men, in the present state of their knowledge, can exercise over Nature so as to modify it for their own advantage, directing their entire forces to this end and regarding social combinations only as means of attaining it" (IV, 550).

Comte's prospectus left the nature of these actions and modifications vague. No doubt for him, as for Saint-Simon, an essential part of this modification was the increased production possible through the development of industry. No doubt Comte also looked to science for the cure of disease and the alleviation of suffering. Comte's optimism about the seemingly endless possibilities for generally improving the conditions of human existence can be seen here, although he expressed that hope in very general terms.

In the preliminary elaboration of the first series which follows this prospectus, Comte concerned himself with working out a method for dealing scientifically with politics. As he did so, certain of his basic premises—about civilization, about history, about science, and about the usefulness of a Positive philosophy—began to emerge. He compared his own "Social Physics" (as he called it at this time) with other attempts to treat politics as a science, and, in the process, was forced to define his own position more clearly. There are important clues to Comte's thought in the relationships he saw between his own theories and those of men like Montesquieu, Condorcet, and Cabanis. Although we have dealt with these "influences" briefly above (see pp. 30–34), the emphasis here will be on Comte's criticisms of these theories.

In the application of scientific method to politics, the first task would be to observe facts, correlate them, and reduce them to general laws. Comte regarded Montesquieu's *Esprit des lois* as one of the earliest attempts to deal scientifically with politics, for in it he "mainly aimed at ranging, as far as possible, under a certain number of heads all the political facts known to him" (IV, 568). Despite his work in observation and classification, however, Montesquieu failed to "perceive that great fact which regulates all political phenomena, the natural development of civilization." Because he paid too little attention to the "necessary succession of the different political states" and placed too much emphasis on what Comte regarded as a secondary matter, the particular form of government, Montesquieu was unable to disentangle himself from "metaphysics." His theory was therefore "dogmatic," in Comte's view, rather than "historical." Montesquieu also exaggerated the influence of "climate," and, because of his concentration on such secondary facts, he was unable to discover the general laws of society's development.

Comte's own belief that social (or political) organizations must be subject to "natural laws" was based on two fundamental ideas. The first of these is that the social organization depends on the general state of civilization. The second idea is that civilization as a whole progresses according to a necessary law. It was Condorcet, claimed Comte, who grasped the general concept that "civilisation is subject to a progressive course, every step of which is strictly connected with the rest by virtue of natural laws; discoverable through philosophic observation of the past, and which determine, in a positive manner for each epoch, the improvements adapted to the social state as a whole, and to each portion of it" (IV, 570).

Condorcet's emphasis on historical development represented a more comprehensive view than Montesquieu's, and his "Sketch of an Historical View of the Progress of the Human Mind" continued the process of giving politics a scientific character. Nevertheless, Comte regarded Condorcet's Classification of the Epochs as unscientific because it was based on an almost arbitrary assumption that each epoch was begun by "some remarkable event, now industrial, now scientific, now political" (IV, 571). Because Condorcet's distribution was not based on "real connections" between facts, no homogeneous series or progression could result. In addition, Condorcet's observations tended to be distorted by his negative view of the past—an attitude which involved him in logical contradictions. On the one hand, Condorcet proclaimed that the civilization of the eighteenth century was superior to its antecedents. This affirmation assumed a total progress which "could only be the sum of the partial advances effected by civilisation during all the preceding states. Condorcet, however, almost always, represents these as having been, from the most essential points of view, periods of retrogradation. We are thus landed in a perpetual miracle, and the progressive march of civilisation becomes an effect without a cause" (IV, 574–75).

The mistakes that Condorcet made regarding the past rendered his deductions about the future erroneous. Condorcet's attempt to predict was justifiable, Comte held, for all sciences aim at prevision. But predictions can only be valid insofar as they are founded on accurate observations and sound deductions. Such prevision is the aim and also the test of science for Comte: "All sciences aim at prevision. For the laws established by the observation of phenomena are generally employed to foretell their succession" (IV, 576). Thus Comte, making his own projections regarding the future, saw himself not as a visionary but as a scientist simply working out the particular consequences of established general laws.

In addition to criticizing Condorcet's Classification of the Epochs, Comte also objected to Condorcet's application of mathematical analysis (that is, the calculus of probabilities) to social science. Despite his own interest in mathematics, Comte insisted that it was not at all necessary to apply mathematical analysis in order to render politics a positive science (IV, 577). Comte held that it would be, in fact, an altogether erroneous procedure for a number of reasons.

First of all, in order to bring any phenomena within mathematical laws, it was necessary that their quantity be fixed. But in physiology (the scientific study of organized bodies), where the phenomena are extremely variable and complex, Comte regarded the application of mathematics as totally impractical in the present state of our knowledge. Such an application would be especially premature, Comte felt, in the case of moral and political phenomena, areas of the most complexity and variability. In the second place, if the application of mathematics were possible, it could only follow the long process of observing and coordinating facts. In the sciences in which mathematical analysis had proved most useful (in astronomy, for example, and physics), it had become so only after the collection of data and the discovery of the general laws governing phenomena. Comte therefore held that the only basis for the establishing of a political science was "direct study," that is, the observation of social-political phenomena and the coordination of these phenomena (IV, 578).

While he admired Condorcet's historical perspective and his insight regarding civilization's progress, Comte built on these ideas in his own way. He preferred his own approach to that of Condorcet for very practical reasons: he believed he could establish a Social Physics on grounds other than mathematics; he believed that moral and political phenomena were too complex and variable to be dealt with mathematically; and he believed that the collection of sufficient data for accurate statistical analysis was too long-term a proposition to be useful in his time.

Another thinker, Cabanis,[2] had tried an alternate approach to "Social Physics." For him, the science of society was merely an extension of physiology. Comte regarded this approach as erroneous too, because it failed to distinguish between the physiology of the race and that of the individual. These two sciences are separate and distinct, Comte insisted.

Comte's approach should be seen in its relationship to these alternatives. He aimed at a scientific study which would begin with the accumulation of distinctly social data. From the correlation of these "facts" Comte hoped to derive the "natural laws" governing society and its progress. From these, he was convinced, he could determine "the real tendency" of civilization.

While nature's laws could not be controverted, such knowledge could give mankind understanding of and power over nature. It could enable mankind to see political regimes not as absolute goods or evils but as relative to the general state of civilization. And furthermore, by demonstrating the general social-political laws, political science could help mankind understand social and political processes so that people might live in harmony with social progress rather than try to establish arbitrary regimes. Such knowledge could help avert or mitigate violent revolutions which occur when obstacles stand in the way of social progress. Such a science, built firmly on "true history," could lead mankind to knowledge of the system "which ought to prevail as the Final Social System" (IV, 589). With scientific knowledge, mankind could work in harmony with nature to avoid not only the violent shocks of revolution, but the quagmires of conflicting opinions.

Even in these early essays, then, Comte began to build upon his basic ideas and to move to a vision of a future society whose outlines might be deduced from the study of the past. The "Final Social System," which represents the perfection of this science, sounds remarkably static in the context of Comte's insistence on history, development, and progress. The "final perfection," however, he was careful to explain, is a somewhat visionary goal—"one which in all likelihood will never be completely attained" (IV, 588–89). None-

theless, as the scientists' knowledge increased, Comte was confident
that the general picture of this celestial city would be filled out in
more and more detail. Although Comte did not here promise that
he would give us a detailed blueprint of the Final Social System,
it is clear that he saw this as the general aim of Social Physics. As
his work progressed and his confidence grew, such a blueprint did
in fact take shape in his *System of Positive Polity*.

III   *The Leadership*

With his fourth essay, "Philosophical Considerations on the Sciences and Savants" (November 1825), Comte focused in on the role
of the intellectuals in restructuring society, and on the adjustments
this group must make in order to become the "spiritual authority"
for the new society. Comte began this essay with a demonstration
of his two fundamental laws. The first of these is the already familiar
"Law of the Three States," which Comte here used to show that
society, having passed through the theological and metaphysical
states, was now ready to complete the transition into what he regarded as its definitive state, based on Positive philosophy. The next
step was to determine the extent to which this transition had been
made and the work which remained to be accomplished. To determine this present status and arrive at his prognosis, Comte worked
from his second fundamental law, that of the classification of the
sciences. Looking back at the history of science, Comte concluded
that the various branches of knowledge had become positive (scientific) in an orderly sequence. The order of their development was
dependent upon the nature of the phenomena, for there are certain
built-in factors which facilitate (or hinder) this process: the greater
or lesser complication of the phenomena, their greater or lesser
dependence on other branches of knowledge, their degree of specialization, and their more or less direct connection with man (IV,
597). The use of these four factors gave Comte a tool for classifying
the sciences which, in his view, not only reflected the historical
development of the branches of knowledge, but which set up a
developmental pattern from astronomy, to physics, to chemistry,
to biology (and physiology).

Just as, somewhat later, the discovery of the periodic law in chemistry gave Mendeleyev a pattern of known elements from which he
was able to predict the existence and characteristics of unknown
elements, Comte's classification created a pattern in which he found

a significant gap—the omission of social phenomena. Since each science developed after the preceding branches of knowledge had reached a certain point, it appeared to Comte that the ground had now been sufficiently prepared for the development of Social Physics. He saw this new science as not only possible, but as the inevitable next step in the process of development. Practical political considerations also convinced Comte of the necessity for Social Physics. Society's present state of mental and moral anarchy was, he held, the result of "the absence of any preponderating system, capable of uniting all minds in a communion of ideas" (IV, 605). Perception of this deficiency led thinkers like de Maistre to advocate a return to the unity of ancient times by subordinating all our conceptions to supernatural philosophy. Such a step backwards was, in Comte's thinking, impossible. Since the "Critical Philosophy," on the other hand, offered no positive grounds for unity, the only alternative was to develop a science of society, a Social Physics, to provide that necessary base. This science, Comte reasoned, would make possible a homogeneous social education, itself the foundation of a stable, well-ordered society.

Having affirmed the necessity for a new scientific basis for social order, Comte turned to the intellectual class from which he expected leadership to come. In the early history of our civilization intellectual leadership had come from the priesthood, the class best provided with the time and facilities for study. Gradually these intellectuals developed methods and theories, first metaphysical and then "positive," which the larger body of conservative theologians found threatening and attempted to suppress. But even rigorous suppression (like the Inquisition, for example) could not stop the inevitable advance of knowledge. Finally, the French Revolution broke the power of the theologians, but, unfortunately, it also left society without adequate leadership, without moral and social unity.

Comte was convinced that the new leadership could come only from the scientists, whose specialized knowledge of the "relations that subsist between the external world and man" might enable them to construct "a system of positive knowledge" as a foundation for the new society. The great obstacle to accomplishing this was the scientists' increasing tendency toward specialization, for this division of labor, which had made possible great advances in science, led to fragmentation rather than unification. In Comte's vision of the future, the task of unification would naturally devolve upon the particular group of scientists investigating social phenomena since this group would be forced, by the dependency of social science on all the preceding sciences (in Comte's hierarchy of the sciences), to deal with the ensemble of knowledge. Comte therefore felt that this group would be in a position to create a unified system of Positive philosophy. While these "savants" were not to be involved in the practical carving out of the technology or the institutions of the new society, they were to have two vital functions: to formulate the generalized positive conceptions underlying the new society and to educate the general public (all levels of society) in the natural sciences. They were, in a word, to be "philosophers," not "engineers."

Comte's desire to play such a role himself was, perhaps, behind his decision not to return to the École Polytechnique. At any rate, he wrote in a letter to his friend Valat that he had never been enthusiastic (*amoureux,* he said) about engineering—whether it concerned itself with bridges or mines. It was only for practical reasons he had let himself be pushed toward these "pitiful careers" (*tristes carrières*).[3] It would seem that the infinitely complex social and political problems were already challenging him to become a political philosopher. Comte, then, early in his career, envisioned the future path of science as leading through social science to a broad overview of human knowledge and human history. This vision is his "first sketch of the problem of the Spiritual Power."

The fifth essay in this group of early works is dated March 1826. In it Comte continued his "Considerations on the Spiritual Power" and dealt further with the need for reorganization of that power. Comte's first concern in this essay was to show the necessity for separating the two elementary social powers, the spiritual (the theoretical) and the temporal (the practical). Comte began, as he so often did, with an examination of history, from which he then deduced certain general laws.

Throughout antiquity, as Comte read its record, all social systems confused these two powers, spiritual and temporal. Consequently, in his view, the greatest triumph of the Middle Ages was the establishment of two separate powers, Catholicism and feudalism, to deal with these two realms. This step was a significant advance for civilization in that it created a spiritual unity transcending national borders. The Feudo-Catholic system was progressive, too, in that it promoted new institutions which replaced the abject submission to authority (or active revolt against it) of the old slave system with a new kind of subordination, clothed at least with voluntary submission. These achievements advanced civilization by making possible a better ordered and a more extended community. Such a community could extend its control over nature and improve the life of its citizens because it created a climate favorable to the development of science and industry.

It was precisely this development of science and industry, however, that led to the decline and eventual dissolution of the theological and military powers. As scientific knowledge grew, it gave man increased power over nature. Gradually the "authority" of science displaced theology. Along with this displacement in the realm of ideas, Comte saw a parallel movement in the practical realm, where industrial development became an alternative to military conquest as a way of getting material goods. As a result of these changes, social disorganization marked the period from the sixteenth to the eighteenth century, when the old dogmas were being challenged by new ones—of unlimited Liberty of Conscience, of the Sovereignty of the People, of Equality. Each step in this historical process represented progress for civilization. Each was useful and, indeed, indispensable. But even as the seeds of the destruction of the Feudo-Catholic system had been carried along within the orderly and peaceful development it had made possible, just so, the critical, negative doctrines of the Revolution carried within themselves the seeds of their own destruction. These revolutionary doctrines, too, were useful and indispensable in their place and time, but they were fundamentally anarchic. In addition, the violent rejection of theological domination led to the view (erroneous, to Comte's mind) either that no spiritual power should exist, or that, if it does, it should be subordinate to the temporal power.

Comte's basic assumptions about history can be seen clearly in this essay. The historian is an objective observer of data. History itself is a record of the progress of civilization, and that process is inevitably (though perhaps irregularly) upward. Progress is measured, in the main, by the increase of knowledge, which gives mankind a better existence in giving him more power over nature. Progress is also measured in part by increased socialization, that is, the creation of stabler, wider social structures within which knowledge (science) can develop and be applied (industry). Further assumptions can be seen in Comte's treatment of the Middle Ages. What was before condemned as dark or barbaric, Comte saw as simple fact to be recorded. In its own place and time each culture was making its own contribution to the inevitable progress of civilization. Consequently, the task of the historian, as scientific observer, should be to deal objectively with the phenomena and to see them always as relative—that is, in the context of their own time and place.

Comte's essay then moves from his sweeping view of the past to the present: to France's symptoms and his own diagnosis. Externally, the symptom is international conflict. Where there was peaceful coexistence under Catholicism, the destruction of the Spiritual Power left nations regulated only by an uneasy, inadequate Balance of Power. Internally, the symptoms are mental and moral anarchy. The questioning of all propositions regarding social good had left no fixed principles for public and private morality: behavior was now governed only by egoism, ambition, expediency. The new institutions, Comte felt, were based on materialism and immediate utility, rather than on a sound, long-range, philosophic foundation. The government, pushed further and further toward the centralization of power, had grown into a monster of bureaucracy. The lack of moral unity had left only two alternatives, force or corruption, and bureaucracy operates systematically through the second of these—corruption. Since Comte's study of history had persuaded him that it was impossible for such conditions to remain as the permanent state of affairs, he concluded that a new Spiritual Power was the only remedy. Only a Spiritual Power could replace anarchy with a new order in which moral superiority would be the corrective regulator of force or wealth.

Having "demonstrated" the necessity for a Spiritual Power, Comte was faced with a number of questions about that power. He divided these into two general sets of considerations: (1) the function of the Spiritual Power and (2) the nature of the organization required to bring it into harmony with modern social conditions. He also promised a concluding essay dealing with the general course by which this reconstruction was to be effected. In this particular essay, Comte treated only the first of these considerations, but it is typical of him that his mind was teeming with future projects.

As Comte began to define the functions of the Spiritual Power, he naturally had as his model the Catholic clergy of the eleventh to thirteenth centuries. Even though the philosophic bases of medieval and modern civilizations differ widely, Comte saw no reason why the functioning of the Spiritual Power could not be similar in the two cases. In his own time, as back then, the Temporal Power should concern itself with *actions*, with the *material* realm: the role of this arm of power was to enforce or prevent actions either by force or by wealth. The Spiritual Power, for its part, should concern itself with *ideas,* with the *mental* realm; it should establish the principles that ought to govern relationships. Through education and "reinforcement by moral means," it should regulate opinion, sentiment, and will. Without returning to retrograde theology, modern civilization must, Comte insisted, produce an appropriate, unified moral system.

Comte stressed the need, on both the national and international level, for a common social doctrine and for a spiritual authority to promulgate that doctrine through education. Only such a nucleus could protect society from the fragmenting forces at work—the limiting isolation of specialization, the selfish ambitions of the materialists, the exploitative force of the military-industrial establishments, the competitive nature of balance-of-power politics. So far as international relations were concerned, the only hope of curbing the "natural rivalry of the nations," Comte warned, was "that furnished by a general doctrine concerning the actual relations of nations, established and habitually proclaimed by a Spiritual Authority which, speaking to each nation in the name of all, finds in such universal assent, the necessary support for asserting its decisions" (IV, 644).

Comte's diagnosis of his age has a twentieth-century, post-Watergate ring: mental anarchy, social materialism, encroaching bureaucracy, and political corruptness. Yet his remedies for the ills frighten us almost as much as the "disease" itself. Comte presented his theories as responses to society's urgent needs and obviously thought he was proposing practical plans. The justification for his whole enterprise was its "utility." While we might agree that order (mental, moral, social, and political) is certainly important, the establishment of "the principles that ought to govern relationships" is by no means as simple as Comte affirmed. Over and above this difficulty are the implications of the proposal that some group should regulate opinion, sentiment, and will, and that this group might have the right to "reinforce" its teachings, even though only by "moral means." Although Comte insisted that the body of belief should be based on the sciences and that this system of Positive philosophy should be the result of general agreement (as we can agree, for example, on the makeup of a molecule of water), our fears are not allayed, for we have yet to see general agreement on matters moral or political. Nor have we succeeded on the international level in creating a League of Nations or United Nations whose "moral influence" is free from political maneuvering, or whose operation is free from the threat of force.

Comte's term *Spiritual Power* is itself somewhat equivocal. The function of the spiritual leaders is educative, primarily, and their teaching is to be based upon the natural sciences. The term, in this context, seems to derive from *esprit* as mind. There are, however, "spiritual" connotations, carried over from Comte's model, Catholicism. For Comte, the term seems to refer not to the other-worldly, but to the moral and social dimensions. The "spiritual" education of the individual would be simply the scientific, intellectual education carried out to its fullest human extent. As the individual came to understand himself and society, the self-seeking instincts would be replaced by the responsible participation of the individual in a well-ordered social structure. The religious connotations of the term are, we submit, somewhat misleading. These connotations are, of course, strengthened by Comte's *later* institution of the Religion of Humanity with all its religious trappings. Comte's use of these essays to prove the consistency of his early and later thought underplays this shift in the meaning of the term *Spiritual Power*. The Religion of Humanity is, after all, a religion. While it does not step off into the supernatural, it represents a step beyond the Spiritual Power of the early works. By the time that Comte got around to investigating the intellectual and moral nature of the spiritual organization (as he promised, at the end of this essay, to do), the scientific observer and hypothesis-maker had become the prophet of a new Religion.

IV   *The Methodology*

The sixth essay that Comte included in this group is his "Examination of Broussais's Treatise on Irritation" (*Journal of Paris*, August 1828).[4] At first glance this work seems out of tune with the other five. Comte's reason for reprinting this essay was markedly personal. Of it he wrote that it "manifests the transition from my social debut to my intellectual career, which began, the following year, with the completion of the course of lectures commenced in 1826, but soon after suspended by my cerebral attack. The insight gained through my personal experience was utilized in this review of the memorable work in which Broussais worthily combatted the metaphysical influence" (IV, Gen. Appendix, iii–iv).

The essay is an interesting document for its insights into the treatment of madness from the point of view of a man who had been through that dark experience. We are reminded that the doctors of Comte's time were still pioneers in the combatting of "metaphysical influence." Physiology was still undeveloped as a science; how, then, could the complexities of psychology and psychiatry be understood? Comte saw Broussais's theory that all illness is caused by the "irritation" (that is, over- or understimulation) of tissues, as an important step in making physiology scientific. Despite its limitations, Broussais's hypothesis represented an attempt to establish a "general law" of pathology. And furthermore, it was based on the "general truth" that "life is sustained only by Stimulation." That is to say, Broussais's theory fitted in with Comte's definition of life, not simply in terms of the organic body itself, but of the living body as subsisting in relationship to its environment. Broussais applied his hypothesis (that disease is an irritation of the tissues) to madness as well. For this special case of irritation in the brain, he proposed prompt and specific treatments to cut short the disease.

Comte was decidedly on the side of the physiologists in their view of mental illness, and he took this occasion to define his own general attitude toward the psychology of the day. The perusal of Broussais's treatise, Comte wrote, "is admirably fitted to avert or cure the contagion of psychology" (IV, 651). Comte shared Broussais's mistrust of the introspective method—"the *pretended metnod* of Internal Observations put forward by psychologists as the basis of the science of man" (IV, 646; italics mine). Comte chided Broussais, however, for not dealing directly enough with this subject, and took the occasion to dispatch this question in a paragraph which is (for Comte, at least) a model of directness (IV, 647).

Comte has often been attacked for refusing to allow that the "introspective method" was a legitimate approach to psychology.[5] He held that the introspective method could give some limited information about the passions and about certain organs, but not about the operation of the thinking organ itself. The mind could not, he maintained, play the double role of observer and observed. Though the introspective method seemed to him faulty, Comte made it clear that he was not, in rejecting it, advocating a return to the reductive mechanistic theories of eighteenth-century scientists, who, like Condillac and Helvetius, for example, "saw in our intelligence only the action of the external senses, disregarding every predisposition of the internal cerebral organs" (IV, 648). But

essentially the study of the mind was, for Comte, a branch of physiology, and it was to be carried out by using the same methods. Like
the living organism of which it is a part, the human mind must be
studied in its inner dynamics as well as in its relationship to external
forces.

Comte's approach to psychology seems particularly wrong-headed
since his emphasis on "external observation" led to an enthusiasm
for the phrenology of Franz Joseph Gall.[6] Here and later Comte
acclaimed Gall's theory relating the capacities and personality of the
individual to the formation of his head. While Gall had, Comte felt,
been mistaken in associating particular functions with certain areas
of the brain, nonetheless Gall had been right in his basic principle—
that all human functions come from particular organs. The study of
head conformations has not, of course, proved as scientific as Gall
and Comte expected.

Comte's review of Broussais's work led to one other "philosophical
reflection" which has a significant place in Comte's later work. In
this essay he defined off, in preliminary fashion, the relationship
between the study of the individual and that of the race. Although
the two are "intimately related," Comte wrote, they are

sufficiently distinct and, above all, sufficiently extensive, to admit of being
separately cultivated, and, therefore, conceived as forming two sciences,
Physiology properly so called and Social Physics. The latter is without doubt
based on the former, which supplies it both with a positive point of departure, and guidance. But it forms no less a separate science, requiring
special observations on the history of the development of human society,
and special methods. It could not, by possibility, be treated simply as a
direct deduction from the science of the individual. . . . (IV, 648)

Comte's approach to social science is clearly defined by his insistence
that the "laws" of social phenomena cannot be predicated on the
"laws" of individual physiology and psychology. He turned to history, instead—the history of social development—there to search
for the general patterns which might be a foundation for the new
science. When it came to the "creation" of sociology—at the end
of the *Cours*—Comte dealt more amply with this distinction between psychology and the newly christened sociology.

Even in his review of Broussais's *Treatise on Irritation*, then,
Comte was not far from the themes of his mature works.

In these essays the young Comte set forth his epic plan. Dantean in scope, his vast, ambitious project took him far afield in time and in topic. As yet, chaos seems to prevail over order, but the motifs which wind through these and future works have begun to form patterns. While Comte was addressing his own time, his essays speak to our concerns in the twentieth century—to our uncertainty about private values and about public morality; to our struggles with materialism, bureaucracy, and corruption. It is quite the opposite, however, with his faith that science could lead mankind out of this wasteland. His confidence seems, at this remove, sometimes touchingly, sometimes irritatingly, naive.

Faith in science underlies his Prospectus, the plan embracing three series of works: (1) the scientific observation of social phenomena (historical and present) from which the general laws of Social Physics may be derived; (2) the establishment of a comprehensive "system of positive education" (i.e., education in the natural sciences), based on these "general laws" (the three stages, and the hierarchy of the sciences); (3) the increased control of man over nature (in accordance with its general laws, to be sure) to lead to a "regenerated society." Visionary as this "regenerated society" seems, Comte held that he was not projecting an imaginary utopia but making a scientific prediction.

Just as these essays set forth Comte's ambitious plan, they reveal the assumptions and premises upon which he operated. Often the essays leave us uneasy. At times Comte's "observed facts" seem to be assumptions or facts selected because they conveniently fit his theories. There is a disturbing circularity, too, in his whole enterprise, in that he began by affirming a need which he then proceeded to fulfill. There are also discrepancies between Comte's view of the historical progress of civilization as "inevitable" and his faith that through science that process can be modified. Even in these early essays there are hints, too, of totalitarianism in the prospect of thought control, of "moral regulation," and of pressure to conform. Yet despite the uneasiness they create, these works also leave us with a respect for the range, discipline, and the dedication of Comte's mind.

Though these early essays received little notice, Comte was now ready to launch out on his own. His first grand project was a lecture series, to begin in March 1826. This course of lectures, in which the early ideas began to be systematized, was interrupted after only three sessions by Comte's illness. The projected series, however, took shape finally as Comte's first major work, the *Cours de la philosophie positive*.

CHAPTER 3

Positive Philosophy:
Old Wine in New Bottles

THE Course in Positive Philosophy, which Comte began in 1826 as a series of public lectures, came to fruition, finally, in the publication of the *Cours de la philosophie positive* in six volumes over a period of years, from 1830 to 1842. Because this work is regarded by many as Comte's main contribution to intellectual history, it is worth examining in some detail.

The aim of the first part (volumes one through three) was to review and systematize all the sciences: each science was to be considered as to its methodology, development, and chief results; each was also to be considered in its relationship to the other sciences. In these volumes Comte developed in exhaustive (and exhausting) detail a number of the concepts which he had sketched out in the early essays. Comte based his systematization of knowledge on what now had become his two general laws: the Law of the Three States and the Classification of the Sciences (into a hierarchy). These "laws" enabled him to approach science as a unity and to create a philosophy of science.

This systematization of knowledge was, however, secondary in the long run to Comte's principal goal, which was to complete the series of sciences by extending scientific methodology to social phenomena. The creation of the new science, Social Physics (or, as it was eventually called, Sociology), was Comte's concern in the final three volumes of the *Course*.[1]

I *"A Great Fundamental Law"*

The opening section of the *Course* naturally picked up many ideas from the early essays. As Comte enlarged upon, reformulated, and

57

unified these ideas, they helped to provide the rationale for the *Course*, and, at the same time, to demonstrate the premises on which Comte's philosophy of science rested.

The rationale was, of course, based upon the usefulness of the work. Comte, convinced that the intellectual anarchy of his time was destroying society, sought to establish through science a basis for general agreement. Only such agreement could, he insisted, restore social order. But if society were to be reorganized on the basis of knowledge (i.e., science), a thorough examination of the present state of human knowledge would be essential. Only so could the validity of science's methodology and its claim to sound knowledge be assessed. Comte believed, furthermore, that the "present state" of knowledge could not be understood without reference to the history of intellectual progress. In order to fill this need for a body of unified knowledge, Comte therefore planned to combine an "anatomy" of each science with a study of its multiple relationships (e.g., to its own development in the past and in the future, and to other branches of science). These two aspects of each science he called Statics (the anatomy) and Dynamics (development). Only an analysis as thorough as this could, he held, place the vast body of new scientific knowledge in its proper perspective. In addition, the turning of scientific method back on science itself would prove once again the usefulness of the method. For Comte, "scientific observation," and it alone, could reveal the patterns of development which make the ensemble of knowledge comprehensible and which make its future course predictable.

Comte was convinced, of course, not only that such patterns exist, but that he had discerned them. The first of these he had begun to formulate as a "general law," the Law of the Three States, as early as 1822 (in the essay "Plan of the Scientific Operations Necessary for Reorganizing Society"). Stated most simply, this first general law described the pattern of intellectual development as consisting of three stages—the theological, the metaphysical, and the positive state. Each phase of this development represented a state of knowledge and a methodology. The process, as Comte described it, begins with the human mind as it first gropes its way toward knowledge— as it seeks to know the essence and the causes of things. Taking its most immediate model, itself, the primitive mind begins by projecting its own image onto the world around. At this stage it attributes everything to animistic spirits (Comte's word for this stage is *fétichisme*), or, somewhat later, to several gods. As the "theological" concept becomes more refined, a single Supreme Being replaces these multiple gods. When, in the course of time, knowledge based on observation increases, belief in these supernatural beings gives way to "metaphysical concepts." At this stage the nature and causes of phenomena are ascribed to abstract forces or entities inherent in the substances. That is, concepts such as "attraction," or "natural right," take the place of the theological explanations, which have now come to seem pure superstition. Further progress leads to the final, or positive, stage. At this point the thinker is no longer interested in the essence of things nor in their first (or final) causes, he has become the scientist, who confines his efforts to observing and classifying phenomena in the hope of discovering the general laws governing those phenomena. Comte's own Law of the Three States was, he felt, scientifically derived from his "observation" of mankind's general intellectual development. He therefore now confidently applied this law to every branch of knowledge, as well as to the intellectual development of every individual and every culture.

II   *"The True Filiation of the Sciences"*

At the same time, it was clear to Comte that all branches of knowledge have not progressed at the same rate. The earliest sciences to develop appeared to him to be those which were the simplest, which dealt with the most general phenomena, and which did not depend upon the prior development of other sciences. From these considerations Comte concluded that there was a "natural order" of the sciences—a hierarchy that would provide a natural and useful classification system. In this system, the sciences fall into two broad general categories: inorganic and organic. Within these divisions Comte ranked the sciences according to their complexity, beginning with the "simpler" phenomena of mathematics, astronomy, physics, and chemistry and moving to the intricacies of the organic sciences, biology (including physiology), and, ultimately, sociology. Comte held that the various sciences had in this order passed from the theological, through the metaphysical, to the positive state.

In Comte's "natural hierarchy" of the sciences each branch of knowledge depends upon the laws and methods of the preceding science, but adds to them. The results are not uniform, however. For, as the complexity of the phenomena dealt with increases, the sciences become less precise and certain. Precision is greatest where the phenomena are simple and where the exactness of mathematical analysis is applicable.

Because of its clarity and preciseness, mathematics had a special place in Comte's hierarchy. For him mathematics represented not just one of the branches of knowledge (like physics or chemistry, for example), but it held a special place as the "first science" and as the basis of the whole of natural science. Other sciences could only aspire to the elegant clarity of mathematics; other sciences could only borrow the tools of mathematical analysis. While Comte valued the methods of mathematics as useful in other fields of knowledge, he also cautioned that "mathematical analysis" ought not to be regarded as the sole scientific tool. Just as the branches of science differ, so the appropriate methods must vary. At each step the phenomena to be dealt with become increasingly complex, and new means of observation and experiment become necessary. In Comte's system, then, each science represented an addition to the sum of knowledge and a contribution to methodology as well.

Comte's view of intellectual progress therefore included both the growing body of knowledge and the increasing capacity of man to deal with complex data. These two elements formed the core of Comte's "positive philosophy," as it was developed in the *Course*. This work is something over and above an exposition of a philosophy of science, however. In it Comte was developing what was to him the only logical system of education. Since he postulated that the individual recapitulates, as it were, the history of the race (HM, 798), it followed that the educational system should be structured along the lines of the history of intellectual development. To study the sciences in the order they have developed would be to see knowledge as a coherent whole. Such a view would enable the student to build his knowledge on the firm base of simple, general phenomena. From there he could reasonably progress to the more complex branches of knowledge. This part of education was to be general in content and addressed to the ordinary student. It would not attempt to deal with the concrete applications nor with the specialized aspects of each science, but would give the general student an overview of human knowledge. This kind of education would aim simply to acquaint the student with the principal "laws" and methodology of each science.

The "course" which he laid out was built upon these premises— that it is important for mankind to understand the ensemble of human knowledge; that it is possible to do so if attention be focused on the progress of that knowledge; that it is essential to keep in mind the broad principles of each branch rather than specific details. In content, then, Comte's educational program was "progressive" in its orientation to science and in its emphasis on the general principles of mathematics and the sciences.

III   *The Laws Applied*

Beginning with mathematics, Comte proceeded to deal systematically with each branch of knowledge in its turn. In each case he set up a definition which would indicate the nature and the scope of the discipline. Then he separated off the "abstract" (in which he was interested) from the "concrete" aspects. This separation enabled Comte to focus on the general principles and "laws" (the abstract elements) which represented to him the real advances made in this particular science. He dealt next with the relationship of this branch of knowledge to others—the way in which it depends on and provides materials for other sciences. Such juxtapositions enabled Comte to compare each science to the others with reference to its usefulness and limitations. From such general considerations, Comte then moved to a specific analysis of each division of the science he was dealing with.

While Comte was very much aware that we are not all destined to be great mathematicians, he insisted on the importance of knowing what each branch represents in the coherent whole of human knowledge. Mathematics, for example, Comte saw as a powerful tool. As the science of "indirect measurement," it provides a useful method for coordinating phenomena in all other fields. In addition, its simplicity and rigor make mathematics a model of clarity and precision. Every discipline, Comte held, aspires to the precision of mathematics (HM, 58).

The second science in Comte's hierarchy is astronomy, the science by which we discover the laws of the geometrical and mechanical phenomena presented by the heavenly bodies. It is a field in which the long process of development can be clearly seen: the centuries-long accumulation of observed data, the application of mathematical analysis to these facts, and, finally, the subsuming of these under a single law. But, for Comte, the achievements of Galileo, Copernicus, Kepler, and Newton teach mankind lessons far more significant than the importance of precision in observation and in logical analysis. The discoveries made by these men demonstrate the confrontation of intellect with all of the forces which oppose progress. The acceptance, finally, of the concept of the double motion of the earth was, for example, an astonishing victory over existing opinions, common appearances, dominating authority, human pride, and theological belief. It was a victory which Comte saw as cause for hope:

No other intellectual revolution has ever so thoroughly asserted the natural rectitude of the human mind, or so well shown the action of positive demonstration upon definitive opinions; for no other has had such obstacles to surmount. . . .
   If the vanity of man was grievously humbled when science disabused him of his notion of his supreme importance in the universe, to this vanity at once succeeded a lofty sentiment of his true intellectual dignity . . . the sound and vivifying conception of Man discovering, by a positive exercise of his intelligence, the general laws of the world, so as to be able to modify them, for his own good, within certain limits. (HM, 157)

Against all odds, then, science substituted for the old theological beliefs a sense of pride in the accomplishments of the human intellect. As the scientist discovered the "general laws of the world," he opened the door not only to an understanding of this world, but to "prevision." And, in Comte's view, an ability to predict with accuracy opened up the possibility that man could modify phenomena.

   Following astronomy in Comte's hierarchy of the sciences is physics, the study of the "laws which regulate the general properties of bodies, commonly regarded in the mass, and always placed in circumstances which admit of their molecules remaining unaltered, and generally in their state of aggregation" (HM, 194). In this field Comte found greater complexity in the phenomena and, consequently, less precise knowledge. There are a number of divisions in this science, which Comte tried to rank in accordance with his general principle, based on the generality and simplicity of the phenomena dealt with. The arrangement he finally set up—barology, thermology, acoustics, optics, electrology—was, as he had to admit, somewhat arbitrary. Still it was, he concluded, a useful arrangement.

   So far as methodology is concerned, physics, like astronomy, depends upon observation and mathematical analysis, but the use of these methods becomes more difficult. For one thing, observation is more complicated in physics because more of the senses are involved. In connection with his discussion of the methods useful in physics, Comte took up the subject of the scientific use of hypothesis. In astronomy, hypotheses were used freely and straightforwardly as tentative theories which explained all the known facts. Comte believed that hypotheses very often facilitated progress as they enabled investigators to look ahead and anticipate results or to postulate general laws. But Comte was careful, at the same time, to stipulate that the use of hypothesis must be subject to certain conditions—the investigator should "imagine such hypotheses only as admit, by their nature, of a positive and inevitable verification at some future time. . . . But . . . if we try to reach by hypothesis what is inaccessible to observation and reasoning, the fundamental condition is violated, and hypothesis, wandering out of the field of science, merely leads us astray. . . . Every hypothesis which strays beyond the domain of the positive can merely occasion interminable discussions, by pretending to pronounce on questions which our understandings are incompetent to decide" (HM, 200). The questions he meant were the old, metaphysical ones—questions about the *nature* of phenomena, "or their *cause*, first or final, or the mode of their production" (HM, 200). It is clear from these statements that Comte was serious about the rigor of scientific method in replacing imagination with observation and reason. Another question of method that Comte regarded as yet to be solved concerned the extent to which the use of mathematical analysis is valid in physics.

In addition to using already established methods, the science of physics developed a new means, experiment, to add to man's resources for study. In the overall picture, this is perhaps the most important accomplishment of physics. For, even though our knowledge is less exact and our power of prevision is less perfect in physics than in astronomy, physics represents a significant advance in human knowledge. It was physics which showed humans how they could, through prevision, modify phenomena (as they, of course, could not do in astronomy). This power of modification also represented another blow to theology because it proved that phenomena are variable, that they are subject (at least in part) to man's will, not just to God's.

Though Comte was far more interested in the methods of physics than in its specific data, he did give a résumé of the major discoveries of modern physics. Prominent among the discoverers were such men as Galileo, Torricelli, Boyle, Descartes, Huygens, Newton, Fourier, Dalton, Bernouilli, Laplace, Volta, Ampère, and Franklin.

These were the men whose investigations into the nature of barology, thermology, acoustics, optics, and electricity had done so much to establish physics as a science. In Comte's time the work was scarcely begun, however. Even by the time Harriet Martineau's translation of the *Positive Philosophy* was published in 1855, her scientific consultant, Professor J. P. Nichol, pointed out the many instances in which great advances in theory or in experiment had taken physics either far beyond Comte's description or in a new and unexpected direction. But such advances did not nullify Comte's work. Indeed, as he himself pointed out, he had "shown what gaps are disclosed in the course of such a survey" (HM, 248). What was essential, in Comte's view, was that man's concepts of the external world had to become scientific as a preparation for the application of science to man himself.

After examining in detail all of the branches of physics, Comte moved on to the next science, chemistry. Chemistry, as Comte defined it, "relates to the laws of the phenomena of composition and decomposition, which result from the molecular and specific mutual action of different substances, natural or artificial" (HM, 252). For chemistry to achieve its aim as a science (i.e., "prevision"), it must, given the "essential properties" of substances, determine the chemical reactions of substances when they are brought together in "well-defined circumstances." Could chemistry but answer these seemingly simple, basic questions regarding the nature and reactions of substances, the information could be utilized in the study of "vital phenomena, the natural history of the globe, and industrial operations." Thus far chemistry's development as a science had benefited man by providing a "rational organization" for other sciences (biology, for example) and for developing technology (industrial operations) (HM, 252).

The immediate difficulty for chemistry was, in Comte's view, its inability to solve the knotty problem of classification. Only as chemists could systematize the rapidly growing body of facts and establish the general laws of chemical behavior would Comte allow that chemistry had attained a truly positive state. To the extent that chemistry could so establish itself, it held the promise of enormous benefits to mankind.

Like physics, chemistry depends upon the preceding sciences in the hierarchy and utilizes all the methods of investigation (observation, mathematical analysis, and experiment) already developed. It adds to them the use of comparison, the study of an extended series of analogous but distinct cases. Comte predicted that this would be a particularly useful method in chemistry, where the elements seem to occur in natural families.

Although the classifications remained yet to be made and the general laws of chemistry to be discovered, Comte saw this branch of knowledge as moving out of the metaphysical into the positive state. Despite its incompleteness, this science, Comte held, could teach us a number of lessons: the usefulness of scientific method (observation, experiment, comparison); the art of "rational nomenclature"; and the ability of man to modify his environment. In addition, it has taught us the perpetuity of matter. However much remained yet to be done in this science, Comte was confident in his own "prevision" of its future accomplishments. He predicted that as soon as chemists could break down substances into their component elements and could succeed in classifying these elements according to their behavior, this science would come of age. [2] Comte saw chemistry as a science which could greatly further human progress as it revealed more about vital phenomena and about the natural history of the globe. Not the least of chemistry's contributions to human progress was its role in the development of industry. For Comte, as for Saint-Simon, progress was defined as the hand-in-hand development of science and industry.

From the science of chemistry, Comte moved naturally to the field of biology and began his study of the living organism by reminding us that man is one biological entity among others in the physical world. While Comte would have agreed with the eighteenth-century view that the proper study of mankind is man, he took care, in the introduction to this section on biology, to point out that the Positivist approaches the study of man from a "scientific" direction:

The study of the external world and of man is the eternal business of philosophy; and there are two methods of proceeding; by passing from the study of man to that of external nature, or from the study of external nature to that of man. Whenever philosophy shall be perfect the two methods will be reconciled; meantime, the contrast of the two distinguishes the opposite philosophies—the theological and the positive. We shall see hereafter that all theological and metaphysical philosophy proceeds to explain the phenomena of the external world from the starting-point of our consciousness of human phenomena; whereas, the positive philosophy subordinates the conception of man to that of the external world. (HM, 301)

Comte's aim in stressing this approach was to make the point that the study of man (and society) was not only a part of his hierarchy of the sciences, but that this part could not be understood save in the context of the whole (organic and inorganic) world.

Despite its importance, the science of biology was still less perfected than chemistry, for the study of living organisms introduces even more complex phenomena. To begin with, it poses the problem of defining life. Comte agreed, basically, with the noted physician, de Blainville, who defined the life of an organism as a "double interior motion, general and continuous, of composition and decomposition" (HM, 306). Comte added, however, that the definition should include not only the condition of a determinate organism but also the idea of a suitable medium (or milieu) in which that organism can exist. The study of *any* living organism must, therefore, take into consideration both internal and external factors.

As was his custom, Comte began with a discussion of the relationship of biology to the other sciences and then turned to the problems of method posed by this particular science. Observation was, as in the other sciences, a principal method in the study of organic life. Various kinds of apparatus (e.g., to improve sight and hearing) had proved useful in facilitating investigation. In addition, this science had profited much by the acquisition of chemical data and the adaptation of its procedures (chemical analysis, e.g.). Mathematical analysis had, however, proved to be of little use in biology so far. Experiment, too, was more difficult to use in this discipline than it was in physics or chemistry. Since a living organism ordinarily does not admit of much alteration of its organs, Comte postulated that only in the modification of the medium in which the organism lives could experiment be of much use. Nature itself, however, provides a kind of "natural experiment" in pathological cases, for study of abnormal cases very often yields knowledge about normal organisms.

The method of study Comte regarded as especially useful in biology was comparison. He systematically sorted out five basic kinds of comparison: between different parts of the same organism; between the sexes; between the various phases in the whole process of development; between the different races or varieties of each species; between all the organisms of the biological hierarchy. Although he was aware that the application of all these methods would still not result in the kind of precision we desire, Comte did envision the possibility of establishing general biological laws certain enough to enable us to predict behavior with confidence.

For the general student, Comte felt that the study of biology would develop two of the most important powers of the human mind: comparison and classification. Through such study the student could grasp the principles of forming natural groups, of coordinating them rationally, and of arranging them into a hierarchy.

From these general considerations, Comte turned to more specific developments in the static ("anatomical") and dynamic ("biotaxic") divisions of biology. Because of its late development (largely in the last half of the eighteenth century), biology was only gradually attaining the "positive" state. From the welter of conflicting theories, Comte sorted out the comparatively recent work which seemed to him to hold the most promise. One of these developments was the shift from the study of organs to tissue analysis. Comte suggested that tissue analysis might be on the way to the discovery of a basic general biological law if scientists should find that they were dealing not with four different kinds of tissue (skin, cartilage and bone, blood, muscle and nerve), but with a single kind of tissue modified by determinate laws.

Another new biological theory which Comte dealt with in some detail was Lamarck's theory of evolution—the theory that organisms are modified under the influence of the environment, and that acquired characteristics are passed on to future generations. Despite his own interest in history and development, Comte disagreed in part with Lamarck. Comte regarded the limits of modification of organisms as very narrow. The wants or needs of an organism might develop latent powers, but they could not, he held, create these powers. Lamarck's theory presuppposes, said Comte, that all of the complex tissues and organs of the highest organism exist in the most rudimentary organism. This assumption Comte was unwilling to accept. He based his own view that the species remain essentially fixed on two grounds: the permanence of the most ancient known species; and the resistance of existing species to the most powerful modifying forces. On these grounds, Comte rejected not only Lamarckian but Darwinian evolution. Comte, instead, formulated his own "general law" that "living species tend to perpetuate themselves indefinitely, with the same chief characteristics, through any exterior changes compatible with their existence. In non-essentials, the species is modified within certain limits, beyond which it is not modifed, but destroyed" (HM, 348). While rejecting Lamarck's theory that acquired characteristics are passed on, Comte did find value in Lamarck's attention to the external influences exercised on an organism. Consequently, Comte's own definition of life stressed the importance of a medium in which the living organism could survive.

Although Comte's examination of the science of biology is more thorough than the above discussion indicates, these examples illustrate the direction of Comte's interests. He was searching, as always, for general laws of behavior. For the living organism, those laws would be determined, in part, by the internal process of development; and, in part, by the interrelationship between the organism and the medium in which it exists.

IV   *The Law's Implications*

Out of his "factual" history of science, Comte developed a comprehensive philosophy of science. From the progress of science he read the progress of mankind as it gained increasing control of the environment and of man himself. Such control was possible only as knowledge reached a "positive" state. That positive state depended first upon observation, then upon the coordination of observed facts and the derivation from these of the general laws which accurately predict behavior. The perception of the relationship of phenomena is the basis of science.

The record of the various sciences developing through the three stages (theological, metaphysical, and positive) suggested to Comte the "natural hierarchy" of the sciences—an order based not simply (empirically) on the historical order of development, but "naturally" and logically on the dependency of certain sciences on others. He stressed always the relative nature of knowledge.

Comte's philosophy of science provided the foundation for his philosophy of education. The educational program he proposed was to be based on the sciences, the only area of certain knowledge and the only study which can increase our control over nature (that is, our voluntary modification of phenomena, internal and external). For Comte the only logical system of study would be to begin with the simplest, most general phenomena, and to acquire one by one the building stones of facts and "laws." At the same time the student would become familiar with the instruments and methods which have enabled mankind to master the more complex branches of knowledge. The hierarchy of the sciences thus provided an outline for education as well as the framework for a philosophy of science.

Comte was aware that this meant an extensive and difficult process of education. Such an education would be, in his view, not an impossible task, but a necessary one. It was one, furthermore, which might be accomplished with the time saved from the "useless study of words, and from futile metaphysical speculations" (HM, 328). Even while Comte presented a philosophy of education, his work, *The Course in Positive Philosophy*, proposed to supply that kind of education. We may well agree with Comte's biographer, Henri Gouhier, that Comte's true vocation was that of educator.

Comte's presentation of the sciences has been variously acclaimed as the major contribution to scientific thought in the nineteenth century and condemned as wrong in detail, incoherent in presentation, and arbitrary in organization. Mill, for example, called this part of the *Course* "that wonderful systematization of the philosophy of all the antecedent sciences, from mathematics to physiology, which, if he had done nothing else, would have stamped him, in all minds competent to appreciate it, as one of the principal thinkers of the age."[3] On the negative side were those like Spencer, who violently rejected both the Law of the Three Stages and the classification of the sciences. Spencer, taking great pains to disassociate his work from that of Comte, held that there are not three methods of philosophizing, but only "one method which remains essentially the same." As for the hierarchy of the sciences, Spencer categorically denied that Comte's arrangement represented either sound history or sound logic.[4]

Perhaps the most significant of Comte's accomplishments in this work was the comprehensiveness of his history of science, defective though his work might be in detail. Whatever its errors and deficiencies, Comte's attempt to systematize knowledge was a step forward from the dictionary-ordering or even of the "family-tree-ordering" of the *Encyclopédie*. It was, indeed, a Napoleonic enterprise—heroic in its scope (encompassing all knowledge) and vision (the implications for the future). It was to the future that Comte himself turned as he began the second part of his work, the task of creating the science of society.

V *The New Science: Methodology*

In the second section of the *Course* Comte completed his hierarchical structure of the sciences. Where the preceding volumes had dealt with the classification of the existing sciences, this part represents the crowning achievement of Comte's enterprise—the creation of a new science, at first called social physics, then finally sociology. Comte was not unique in his desire to make positive man's knowledge regarding social phenomena, for, as we have seen, other major thinkers (among them Montesquieu, Condorcet, and Saint-Simon) had tried to do so. It was Comte, however, who took the root idea that social phenomena must be subject to general laws and designed a methodology and a systematic theory whereby he could begin to sketch out the new science.

In setting up the philosophic base of sociology, Comte again stressed the urgent need for a solution to the anarchy of his day and reiterated his conviction that only in science could there be found a sure foundation for belief and action. As we have seen, Comte was convinced that the moral and political anarchy of his day had its source in the intellectual confusion that came from the conflict between the outmoded remnants of theological and metaphysical thinking. The result of this unresolved conflict was society's oscillation between the claims of order and the claims of progress. Comte's theory was that if we could but understand the role that each of these successive modes of thinking had played in the history of man's social progress, then mankind might find (or create) an organization able to reconcile the conflict between order and progress. Society could then resolve its problems, and not simply doctor the symptoms of disorder. The proposed solution must, of course, have its proper scientific foundation of observed facts and tested theory. If it were indeed possible to discover from the data the general laws governing social phenomena, then, Comte claimed, man might not only understand the general divisions of society, but he could learn, as he had in the other sciences, to modify social phenomena within those laws. The social organism could thus manage, for example, to aid useful or favorable tendencies and to avoid useless or dangerous actions. Comte believed, of course, that he had discovered these general laws and that this knowledge would make possible the reconciliation of order and progress.

To arrive at those general laws, Comte used the materials already developed in the sciences preceding this in the hierarchy. Sociology could only now make its appearance, for only recently had the other sciences, particularly the biological sciences, developed sufficiently to provide the base necessary for a social science. We have seen the importance of this base in biology, where Comte had insisted on the vital relationship between the living organism and the medium in which it existed. Such an emphasis showed the necessity of understanding both the organic and the inorganic sciences. Similarly, sociology could not exist until knowledge about the most complex forms of both inorganic and organic phenomena had become scientific. The developments Comte had recorded in chemistry, physics, biology, physiology, and psychology led him to suppose that it was time to take the next step. Furthermore, in the study of social phenomena themselves a broad base of observations and tentative theories now seemed to provide an adequate foundation for the new science.

Although the new science depended particularly upon the materials of biology and began where the upper reaches of biology left off, it presented its own special problems. In the first place, Comte warned that the laws of sociology could not just be carried over from physiology or psychology, for he saw man in society as generating something independent of individual human will—forces distinctively collective. In addition to this, the new science promised to be extraordinarily complex. If scientists were finding it difficult to understand individual human beings, how could they presume to grasp phenomena involving masses of human beings, vast movements, and great stretches of human history. And finally, if the laws of individual human behavior were, as Kant suggested, not precisely determinate but "statistical" in nature, how much more indeterminate would be these infinitely more complicated phenomena of social behavior. Even while Comte acknowledged all of these difficulties and accepted the idea that knowledge of social phenomena could never be as precise as he might desire, he still believed that the regularities were sufficient to enable mankind to predict and to modify the actions of society.

The special problems posed by social physics entailed certain modifications in method. Since the basis of any science is the observation of facts and the coordination of them into general laws, social physics, too, must be so grounded. The other methods of experiment and comparison would have their uses in the social science as in the preceding sciences. In the adaptation of these methods to the new science, however, each is modified somewhat. Observation, for example, is made difficult because of the vast range and complexity of the phenomena. Here, more than anywhere else in the realm of science, the observer needs a theory or hypothesis to guide him in connecting the facts. While the investigator may find analogy and a priori theories useful, Comte stressed that such devices must always be used carefully and must always be subjected to verification. Experiment, too, would doubtless be more difficult in social physics than in the physical sciences. Nevertheless, here, as in biology, nature provides certain abnormal states ("diseases" or disturbances of the social organism) which might work as the equivalent of laboratory experiments. Such pathological cases might be regarded as variants which shed light on normal forms and functions. Comparison, Comte thought, would be an especially useful method of study and could be used in various ways—within a society or "anatomically" (as in biology), cross-culturally, or historically. All of these comparisons could help us understand social relationships: the relationship of parts within a society, the relationship of a particular culture to other cultures, or the relationship of a culture to other stages of its own existence.

Comte saw particular promise for sociology in the study of historical relationships. He therefore developed a special approach, the "historical method," which he called the chief device of sociology: "it is the only basis on which the system of political logic can rest" (HM, 481). It seemed to Comte so important a method that he developed it as a fourth and separate mode of scientific research (HM, 485). The "historical method" is, as Comte defined it, "the rational use of social series," that is,

. . . a successive estimate of the different states of humanity which shall show the growth of each disposition, physical, intellectual, moral, or political, combined with the decline of the opposite disposition, whence we may obtain a scientific prevision of the final ascendency of the one and extinction of the other,—care being taken to frame our conclusions according to the laws of human development." (HM, 482–83)

History was, for Comte, the process of social evolution—"the necessary influence of human generations upon the generations that follow, accumulating continuously till it constitutes the preponderating consideration in the direct study of social development" (HM, 481). To approach historical facts without this sense of interconnection and filiation would be to reduce them to a mass of meaningless facts and confused descriptions. "Historical analysis" must, like other scientific methods, be used with care. We must, Comte wrote,

employ it first upon the past, by endeavoring to deduce every well-known historical situation from the whole series of its antecedents. In every science we must have learned to predict the past, so to speak, before we can predict the future; because the first use of the observed relations among fulfilled facts is to teach us by the anterior succession what the future succession will be. (HM, 483)

Since the complexity of the facts makes his task extraordinarily difficult, Comte added, the investigator using this historical method must carefully verify his observations and also check his theories against the laws, physiological and psychological, of individual human nature. Such care should help the researcher avoid errors of observation and logic which can be so easily obscured by the mass of complex material.

Comte's historical method combines observation (historical facts) with mathematical concepts (rational use of social series, deduction). Its basic premise is the concept of progress, and the method proved particularly useful when Comte was dealing with the dynamics of sociology, the aspect which interested him the most.

VI *"The Spontaneous Order of Human Society"*

Having established the methodology he regarded as appropriate and useful, Comte began his analysis of society. With this science as with all the others, Comte dealt with both its static and dynamic aspects. His study of society begins with "social statics"—an anatomy of society which takes up, in turn, the conditions of social existence for society's three basic elements: the individual, the family, and the society.

In Comte's discussion of the individual and of the human attributes which give society its fundamental character, psychology and sociology mesh together. He focused his attention on two facets of human nature which seemed to him relevant to the development of society. First, the predomination in human beings of "affective impulses" (of instincts and feelings) over the intellectual faculties means that it takes some strong and constant stimulus to force man to use his reason. Hence the mental activity which leads to development (or progress) is not the work of the majority, but of a few individuals. Comte's second observation regarding human psychology was that the lowest, most personal (or selfish) instincts tend to predominate over man's nobler, social (or altruistic) ones. From these observations Comte concluded that we cannot rely on either a general appeal to reason (such as we associate with the Enlightenment, for example) or to the social instincts (such as we associate with Shaftesbury or the sensibility movement) to create or to hold together a society. Because human nature tends to be indolent and self-seeking, all notions of public good must be based upon private advantage. Comte seems to have aligned himself here with the Utilitarians, but he was unwilling to reduce human nature to simple self-interest. There were, he believed, two moderators of the human tendency to indolence and egotism: intellectual activity and social institutions. The process of socialization depends on the cultivation of these forces.

Bridging the gap between the individual and society is the basic social unit, the family. Within this unit, there are two orders of relationships: the sexual union, and the rearing of children. Comte's views regarding both of these relationships were conservative and based on the idea of hierarchy. While Comte agreed that the position of womankind was degrading and unfair, he was totally out of sympathy with the feminist movement of his day (HM, 504) and regarded the equality of the sexes as "incompatible with all social existence" (HM, 505). Women are inferior in certain respects to men, he wrote. They are less fit for intellectual activity or government. Man is therefore the natural head of the social unit. Women are, however, more sympathetic and social than men. That is to say, women represent the power of love, the noblest kind of power. Their chief functions should therefore be found in their roles as mothers or as moderators of social forces. Between husband and wife there is consequently a "natural" division of labor: the functions of each sex are appropriate to the natural capabilities and temperament (as Comte saw them) of that sex.

In the second kind of family relationship, that between parent and child, the "natural subordination" is a function of age and experience rather than of sex. Comte saw family relationships as providing a model for government units in their example of spontaneous obedience to authority. Such obedience was without degradation because it was based on gratitude; such "natural" authority was absolute, but tempered by affection and geniality.

The "critical doctrines" of the eighteenth century were, Comte felt, destructive to both kinds of family relationships. To allow divorce was to attack the foundations of the socializing institution of marriage. In addition, the new emphasis on education took children away from their parents' guidance at an early age and tended to undermine that social model provided by the home. The sense of family had been further eroded, Comte argued, by the abolishment of hereditary rights to property. Comte maintained that the family should be strengthened as a social force, not weakened. Marriage ought to be indissoluble, and the "natural hierarchy" of authority clearly established. After all, the family provides the child with the first and strongest sense of social cohesion—a cohesion built on social affection and mutual reponsibility. It is the unit, too, which represents social continuity—a continuity which ties the present to the past and to the future.

The third element, society, Comte treated in very general terms. It is an association (versus the "union" in marriage), organized on the basis of a division of labor. This distribution of employment contributes to social stability, Comte claimed, because it permits the development of individual capacities. Such channeling could also have negative effects, however, for it encourages narrow specialization and the cultivation of private or class interests. Society must therefore guard against such dispersive tendencies.

Comte came, at this point, to his basic theory of government. The primary function of government is to create a feeling of the whole. If it is to create this sense of unity, it must operate more in the intellectual and moral realm than in the material. According to Comte, it is not the government's business to bring about progress, but to maintain order, which, in turn, permits development. As a society develops, however, the role of government becomes more important. Progress comes naturally as a result of the division of labor, which makes possible the intellectual and technical development essential to society's advance. But, as the social unit becomes larger, and as the division of labor increases, the government must expand and forcefully cultivate the sense of community.

In the overall view of society, then, each of the three elements— individual, family, and society—has to be considered. At each level there are certain functions relating to socialization: personal morality involves the disciplining of the personal instincts; domestic morality, the cultivation of the social (or sympathetic) instincts; and social morality, the special development of the intellect. Thus Comte perceived even social statics in terms of the processes by which socialization is (or should be) accomplished. In this work Comte made no attempt to anatomize society in a full sense. He himself commented on the condensed and abstract nature of his sketch of social statics.

VII   *The Natural Progress of Human Society*

Comte focused his attention instead on "social dynamics," the aspect of social science which really caught his interest (HM, 463). The tendency of Comte's mind was, as ever, to "expatiate o'er all the scene of man" and to absorb all into his system. As a consequence, Comte's interpretation of history is an impressive accomplishment in the creation of a philosophy of history, however much we may quarrel with the particulars of it, or even with the basic premises which are our concern here.

The first of Comte's premises is the concept of progress, an idea which had come into wide, though hardly universal, acceptance in the eighteenth century. While people had to admit there had been progress in such things as science and technology, there were those who questioned the applicability of this idea to the arts, to moral sensibility, and to fundamental human intellectual capacities. Comte simply assumed the argument was settled. We are generally in agreement, he wrote, that there is progress in human affairs; the only question is whether or not it is subject to invariable natural laws. Comte's response to this question was simply that the scientist could hardly believe otherwise (HM, 464).

Comte then set up his basic definition of progress in civilization: it is the increasing preponderance of the human (that is, the intellectual and social) over the animal qualities in man. From there, Comte went on to sketch an outline of social progress by comparing it to the development of the individual organism. Man moves from his social infancy, where his main concern is personal (subsistence and survival), to a social "adolescence," where his sexual instincts lead him into a domestic, then parental, relationship. The responsibilities connected with being a husband and then a parent make the individual plan for the future and hence cultivate social maturity in the individual. As social feelings and intellect are developed, the individual is ready to enter into a larger association advantageous to all. Comte explained the development of society, in a similar way, as a "natural growth" out of the selfish, instinctive concerns related to the family's survival. From this family-unit base there develops, through intermarriage, the broader tribal unit. Both family and tribe demonstrate in a natural way the value of cooperative effort. Furthermore, Comte continued, the natural division of labor within these groups makes possible the specialization and efficiency which encourage the development of the larger associations we call societies. A society progresses as man's actions on his environment increase and as the individual is freed from want. In the advanced society each person is free to develop his unique capacities, and, in particular, his intellect.

We now come to the second of Comte's premises—that it is the intellect which is the index of progress. Comte called intellectual development a "key" only and promised to check this against other aspects of progress—material, moral, and aesthetic development, for example. He did, in fact, refer at times to certain other evidences of amelioration: the refining of customs and manners, the improvements in social organization, the progress of the arts. Such advances were, however, much less significant to Comte than mankind's intellectual development, and especially the scientific advances which enabled man to act on his environment. The real history of society was, for Comte, the record of the developing mind: its beginnings in instinct, its strengthening in practical common sense, its flowering in science.

Another of Comte's premises was the idea of human perfectibility. The term refers not to some utopian ideal (for the individual or for society), but to an ongoing process. Comte assumed that there was some instinct in man which urged him "to develop the whole of his life, physical, moral, and intellectual, as far as his circumstances allow" (HM, 463). Just as the individual always pushes against the limits of his circumstances, each social state is as "perfect" as its external environment and its internal conditions allow. For Comte (as later for Taine) the key to understanding an individual or a social group was the complex interrelatedness of the inner dynamics of the organism and the external factors of time and place. Such a formulation stresses the relativity of social phenomena. Social groups, institutions, and political organizations are not abstract entities in Comte's view, but must be seen as interrelated parts of a whole civilization. Thus a society's intellectual, aesthetic, moral, and physical activities can only be understood in the context of its time, in relationship to prevailing institutions, manners, and ideas, as well as in its responses to its physical environment.

Since Comte emphasized the relativity of social phenomena, he had to define with care his grounds for judging that one society is better than another, or improved over a previous stage. A society progresses, he claimed, insofar as it fulfills three conditions, that is, when it manifests (1) an increased action on the environment through the advancement of the arts and sciences, (2) an amelioration in customs and manners, and (3) a gradual improvement in social organization. When a society functions well, the wants of the people are better satisfied and the population tends to increase. In addition to these material evidences of progress, there are also the opportunities the improved society offers the individual for intellectual and moral development (HM, 467).

Comte's final major premise is that social phenomena, though governed by natural laws, are modifiable. While this may seem paradoxical, it is, of course, the justification for his whole work. The primary function of science being, in his view, to predict and to enable man to modify phenomena, the function of social science could be no different. In fact, the very complexity of the phenomena represented to Comte not so much the difficulty of understanding phenomena, but the hope of manipulating them—always within the framework of the "natural laws" governing them. While Comte felt, for example, that "natural laws" dictated the order of society's stages of development, he maintained that an understanding of social laws and social goals could enable a society to bring about favorable changes more quickly or help it to avoid "useless or dangerous" actions.

A frequent criticism of Comte is that he did not really accomplish what he set out to do—that he did not really create a "science of society." Such criticism ignores the fact that Comte himself stressed that science was not yet advanced enough for a "concrete sociology" since the work of collecting, classifying, and analyzing data remained yet to be done. And, because there were still great gaps in many areas of knowledge (in the related fields of geography, geology, and biology, for example), a "concrete sociology" would necessarily be the work of the future. Comte further claimed that his special endeavor was only to provide a viable hypothesis, a sociological theory which would make sense of the vast body of facts already available. Every science, he pointed out, demonstrates the need for hypothesis. A scientific hypothesis serves to advance science insofar as it replaces the aimless collection of miscellaneous facts with an orderly and meaningful process. Because a theory postulates a certain relationship between facts, it makes possible a systematic collection and analysis of data and gives the scientist's inquiry direction toward a specific end (proving or disproving the hypothesis). Even should the particular laws he postulated prove not to be correct, this method, Comte claimed, was the right approach. Comte's own "creative task," as he saw it, was to provide such a theory for sociology (HM, 544).

As Comte began to apply his hypothesis to the history of mankind, he carefully limited his project by specifying that his focus was to be on abstract rather than concrete sociology—that is, he planned to deal as a rule with only the most general phenomena rather than with exceptional events or minute details. He would, in fact, have preferred to give us an "abstract history," without the names of men, or even of nations, were it not that such particulars might help clarify his ideas. Comte was aware, too, that to trace the development of the most advanced civilization (French, of course) from the primitive conditions of its beginnings would require a disciplined mind fixed upon general phenomena and general laws. But Comte was never one to be daunted by the prospect of rigorous, sustained effort. Comte reminds us, finally, that this kind of mainline endeavor presents great difficulties not only because there are many enticing byroads, but because progress in various fields has been unequal. Just as in his own day theological, metaphysical, and scientific thinking coexisted, there had been in every preceding period an admixture of these "successive" states. Comte's solution of this problem was to define the nature of a period by that which seemed to him to have dominated the moral and social ideas of that particular time. Having thus clarified his approach and methodology, Comte turned to history itself and began to examine the stages of civilization much more completely than he had before. Beginning with man as cannibal and fetish-worshiper, Comte tried to define the main characteristics of this (and each successive) stage and to sort out the civilizing forces at work. Comte sought his key to the future in an understanding of the past.

The hypothesis Comte brought to the study of man's history was, of course, his theory of the three stages: theological, metaphysical, and positive. These general categories he now subdivided further so that he might more clearly trace the development of civilization. He stressed always the abstract nature of his "history"—even when dealing with what seem to us historical cultures, such as those of Egypt, Greece, or Rome.

Because knowledge about the early state of mankind was so limited, Comte eked out the sociological facts by appealing to our general knowledge regarding individual human development. Refusing to accept the Rousseauean notion that the childhood of the race was a "golden age," Comte pictured early man as primitive, self-seeking, cannibalistic, and fetishistic (i.e., as man begins to be conscious of the world outside himself, he "conceives of all external bodies as animated by a life analogous to his own") (HM, 545). In a world peopled by human beings dominated by instinctive feelings and powerful imaginations, only certain kinds of activities, Comte reasoned, are likely to progress. While strong feeling and imagination are qualities favorable to the development of the fine arts, these traits work somewhat against intellectual development. Furthermore, fetishism itself is a "feeble instrument" of intellectual progress, Comte felt, because the gods are too individual or local to provide either the unity of belief or the priesthood which might assist in such development. Although man's conquest of nature began during this period (in the taming of animals, the use of fire, and the invention of tools), fetishism is essentially fatalistic and therefore somewhat unfavorable to the development of "industry" (HM, 553).

From the wandering existence of this carnivorous creature, man, whose "first action . . . on the external world must [have been] in the form of devastation" (HM, 556), it was a long road to a settled, civilized society. Theology, no doubt, played a part in this shift insofar as it kept certain aspects of nature sacred, and as it imposed its sanctions or taboos regarding certain kinds of behavior. At any rate, it was only as fetishism gave way to polytheism that larger social units—with all their advantages and disadvantages—tended to form.

In this second phase of civilization, the development of polytheism itself indicates that men had begun to generalize likenesses. Where, in fetishism, worship is directed to "objects which are nearest and commonest," the gods of polytheism are of a more general and abstract character. This capacity for generalization reflects a certain intellectual progress, but along with it there also came other significant accomplishments: the development of mathematics in Egypt, and the beginnings of natural science in Greece. Art, too, continued to flourish under polytheism and to contribute vitally to social feeling.

The evolution of larger social units meant that society became more structured. Comte points out that certain "natural" divisions of labor began to occur: a priesthood became the intellectual, speculative class; women became more confined to a domestic role; slaves, acquired through the main activity of the time, war, provided a class of laborers.

Although Comte did not hesitate to condemn war and slavery for his own time, he looked at these practices somewhat differently so far as the ancient Egyptians, Greeks, and Romans were concerned. In the context of those times, Comte claimed, war played its part as a socializing influence. The pressures of war, for example, forced man early on to develop tools. War was an important factor, too, in the progress of mechanical and chemical technology. Apart from such material progress, war also helped to consolidate the social group—to cultivate the in-feeling which contributes much to order. Furthermore, success in war enlarged the social unit and thereby forced many of the changes in society which make for progress. And finally, through slavery, war forced the defeated to turn toward industry.

The slavery of those times, unlike the "shameful anomaly" of nineteenth-century slavery, even had, in Comte's view, certain positive values. In the first place, it was a mitigation of the practice of killing one's enemy. In the second place, said Comte, it was the means of educating, disciplining, and developing a settled labor force which in the future was to provide an alternative to war as a way of getting material goods. This view of war and slavery demonstrates Comte's "objective" view of the past as well as his relativistic evaluation of phenomena.

Within polytheism Comte differentiated three main phases: Egyptian, Greek, and Roman. The first of these was predominantly theocratic and demonstrates the development of the "universal base of ancient civilization"—a caste system. Where the strength of such a theocratic society was stability and order, the Greek and Roman civilizations were oriented to expansion and conquest. Rome's great accomplishment, for example, was to conquer, assimilate, and consolidate its expanding empire. Its success in establishing a vast governmental system and a wide communication network throughout the Roman Empire prepared a setup within which monotheism could operate to create a greater unity. In addition, the power base of the rulers—force—had begun to be challenged by those who thought the world ought to be governed by mind. In this challenge Comte discerned the germ of a separate spiritual power, which was eventually to play against the power of the military leaders. It was precisely by the cultivation of this spiritual power separate from the temporal that the next phase, monotheism, fashioned the "universal morality" necessary to unite diverse nations.

While Comte regarded the development of the intellect as the index of progress, he rejected as dangerous and utopian the Aristotelian idea that philosophers ought to be kings. "The real social office of mind is . . . to modify, by its consultative or preparatory influence, the rule of material or practical power, whether military or industrial . . ." (HM, 601). It was not the function of the mind, then, to rule in the world of action, but to educate and to cultivate social feelings. The introduction of this kind of spiritual power, separate from the temporal, was, in Comte's view, the chief achievement which enabled Medieval Catholicism to develop into so great a power.

For its part, the temporal power of the Middle Ages gradually took the shape of feudalism. As the chief care of the Roman Empire had become its own preservation, military power became primarily defensive, and its forces were dispersed under feudal lords. With the decline of conquest, the supply of slaves became more limited, and a system of hereditary serfage took its place. This system took on a somewhat nobler character as it was modified by the ideals of chivalry: the conquering warrior became instead the staunch defender, the feudal proprietor, and the director of agriculture. Gradually the shift from military action to settled work led to industrial progress and eventually to the emancipation of the serf. Feudalism represented, to Comte, a transitionary state, whose function was to prepare for modern industrial society.

While the feudal system regulated temporal existence, Catholicism was gradually gaining more ascendancy. In doing so, Catholicism succeeded in transcending national boundaries, even those of the Roman Empire itself. Because the organization and functions of Catholicism provided the models for the spiritual direction of Comte's proposed Positivist state, we need to look at them to see what important social needs they met.

In the first place, the organization of the Church impressed Comte with its effectiveness. For one thing, the vast scope of the Church's operation made it a truly international organization. The hierarchy of the Church also broke down other boundaries—those of caste. The clerical system, Comte held, was an open one, based on merit. Celibacy further ensured the breakup of hereditary caste systems. In addition to these advantages, the monastic institutions provided the tight communities which enabled the Church to cultivate discipline, moral ideals, intellectual development, political aptitude, and a historical sense. Finally, the Church hierarchy, reaching from lay brother to Pope, represented a separate and independent state, unified in belief because of its final authority—the infallibility of the Pope.

In the second place, the Church provided unifying beliefs, education, and worship for the vast community it served. While the Church's intellectual base was weak, says Comte, it was better than that of the military leadership—at least it provided for religious instruction and social development. Comte's major criticisms of the Church concerned the intellectual weakness of its dogmas. Nevertheless, he conceded that even these faulty doctrines had their necessary functions. For example, Comte regarded the doctrine of the fall of man through Adam as "morally revolting," but necessary as an explanation of human suffering (HM, 615). So, too, the view that Catholicism is the sole way to salvation arouses moral indignation, yet it also helped to sustain the unity of the Church (HM, 614–15). The Church's insistence on absolute faith and its consequent repression of all dissent represented its most vigorous attempt to impose unity. Comte was willing to concede that such rigorous control might be "dangerous perhaps," yet he insisted that the Church's actions were not only necessary, but, indeed, "a real advance" (HM, 614).

Finally, through its sacraments and worship services, the Catholic Church succeeded in joining the individual to a "universal" system. The sacraments served to socialize the individual by reminding him periodically of this connection. The Mass suppressed the bloody sacrifices of previous times even while it satisfied, through the symbolic act, the "instinctive need" for sacrifice. Furthermore, the focal figures of Catholicism provided "ideal models" for mankind: Christ, in whom "all the perfection that they could imagine in human nature" was concentrated; and the Virgin, "a yet more ideal conception . . . [of] the feminine type"—a woman in whom purity was reconciled with maternity (HM, 626).

The genius, then, of Catholicism was its creation of a suitable moral power which raised people out of selfish interests to general and permanent ones. The Church gave expression to the people's "most general and permanent needs . . . in a form of universal doctrine," and invested those needs "with sanctity in real life, individual and social" (HM, 624).

The seed of weakness within this "masterpiece of human wisdom" was its failure to incorporate intellectual progress into itself. Although it had fostered an intellectual class (the priesthood), Ca-

tholicism did not readily accept intellectual advances, and, after ten
centuries of rising power and two of dominance (the twelfth and
thirteenth), it became defensive and retrograde. (Comte dated the
beginning of the Church's decline from the fourteenth century.) The
process of dissolution simply made clear the defects of the Feudo-
Catholic system: Comte saw Protestantism and the critical doctrines
of the Revolution not as a cause, but as an effect of decay. Nevertheless, what Comte felt was destined to expire was only the doc-
trinal part of Catholicism, not its organization: ". . . reconstructed
upon a sounder and broader intellectual basis, the same constitution
must superintend the spiritual reorganization of modern society
. . ." (HM, 636). Clearly, Comte himself intended to reconstruct
this "masterpiece of human wisdom" on a sounder basis.

As the old Feudo-Catholic order faded and yielded place to the
new (the Metaphysical stage), there were three major forces at work
to bring about this change: the intrinsic weaknesses and contradictions of the Feudo-Catholic order itself; the "critical" attacks on the
part of Protestants and Deists; and the development of science and
industry, associated by Comte with the rise of the Positive system.
In the Metaphysical stage, the attack on the old order began in
earnest when theological explanations of phenomena were aban-
doned as unsatisfactory and began to be replaced by abstract terms
(such as attraction, ether, and affinity)—terms not yet scientific, but
tending in that direction.

The radical weaknesses of the old order began to appear as early
as the fourteenth century. The Church's resistance to intellectual
progress became apparent when Pope Boniface tried to dominate
all thought, and the Church's efforts to suppress heresy became
more and more violent. Protestantism, from the first individual
thought to Luther, to Deism, and to atheism, represented to Comte
different forms of protest against the intellectual ban imposed by
the Catholic and feudal order. These various protest movements
challenged the old powers on a number of issues, but their work
was essentially "critical" and "negative"—that is, they did not represent a new constructive system which might be substituted for
what they undermined. While Comte agreed that the right to free
inquiry was essential for scientific progress and that the emphasis
on individual responsibility fostered independence, he had little
patience with most of the critical doctrines. Comte held, for example, that the right to "private judgment" led only to vanity; that
the claim to "equality," far from being realizable, could only foster

pride and envy; and that the call for the "sovereignty of the people" encouraged an ambition which could only be self-seeking (HM, 672). The main thrust of Comte's criticism was that these doctrines never cultivated social virtues; they only promoted an individualistic self-seeking which inevitably threatened to dissolve any social order.

On the secular side, industrial development had begun to shake up the feudal system as well. The growth of commerce and industry had been stimulated by certain mechanical inventions (the compass, the printing-press, and firearms, for example) and by maritime discoveries (of the New World and of a new route to India). Not only had industry become the basis of military power, but the urban, industrial community was becoming a political power unit rivaling the monarch and the aristocracy. Eventually the rapid development of technology in the eighteenth century made possible the great spread of industry, which was to Comte the most characteristic feature of modern civilization.

Comte (like others in his time) was particularly interested in the phenomenon of industry. He defined its character as "the systematic action of Man upon the external world, guided by the knowledge of natural laws" (HM, 705). While Catholicism held its ground, man's action upon the world had been limited because it was regarded as dangerous to tamper with God's providence (HM, 706). Under Protestantism, however, the encouragement of individual enterprise and self-reliance permitted more freedom to act upon the world. Other factors contributory to industrial growth were the division and, gradually, the organization of labor in more efficient ways. Perhaps the most significant development in the eighteenth century was the coalition between science and industry, and the tremendous changes emerging from the resultant technology.

While other theorists emphasized different aspects of industry— for example, the hostility between workers and owners or the dangers of (or necessity for) free enterprise—Comte looked on industry as the most effective way to accomplish what man is put here to do: to act upon the external world in accordance with natural laws. Even the concentration of capital in the hands of a few seemed to Comte not a cause for alarm, but, on the contrary, evidence that a more efficient management of industry was evolving. Despite the obvious need for a fairer distribution of goods and for the mitigation of exploitative greed, Comte was confident that industry, regulated not by law but by a new spiritual power, could provide the temporal leadership of the new Positivist state. Already in the seventeenth and eighteenth centuries, the power of industrial wealth and numbers had begun to challenge the traditional political power of monarch and (military) aristocracy.

Although Comte stressed the negative aspects of the Metaphysical stage, he also traced the rise of the "positive system" and the intellectual progress made throughout the period. Major contributions had, he felt, been made by the founders of positive philosophy, Galileo, Descartes, and Bacon, each of whom set a different path for those who followed. Galileo extended science, while Bacon and Descartes showed the necessity for a new philosophy. Descartes's approach to philosophy was more scientific and systematic than that of Bacon, and more oriented to inorganic science. Bacon's work was more vague and social—important in the study of man and society. Unfortunately, followers of Descartes and Bacon created two erroneous systems (the one French and the other English), each of which failed to deal with organism and medium (man and the external world) as an integral whole.

In Comte's estimation, the most significant philosophical idea to emerge in this period was the "great concept" of human progress. Although important work had been done in the individual disciplines—in mathematics, chemistry, and the rudiments of biology—science was becoming more and more specialized, and hence increasingly fragmented despite the progress it had made.

Comte summed up the period as one of "damaging speciality" in industry, in art, in philosophy, as in science. In no area was there an organizing theory or even an awareness of need for one. Because of the lack of direction and of coordinated effort, society merely existed in a state of confusion, crisis, and anarchy. It was this diagnosis that led Comte to his prescription for the renovation of society—a prescription he believed would create the unity of belief and purpose essential for a healthy society.

Comte has justifiably been called "the sociologist of human and social unity." Whether we turn to his classification of the sciences or to his law of the three stages, the emphasis on unity is the same. Comte carried these same organizing principles into his sociology—the statics analyzing the structural organization of society; the dynamics tracing the single curve of civilization's development. His prescription for the ills of society, too, was predicated on the need for unity, and in the final section of the *Course* Comte outlined some of the basic ways in which Positivism could fill this need.

The first step toward the achievement of social unity was, in Comte's view, the creation of a unified set of beliefs. Comte believed that Positivism offered a science-based philosophy with which no reasonable man could take issue. Rejecting the individualistic "rights" claimed by the "Protestants," Comte laid stress instead on the duties of the individual. One such duty was to deal positively (i.e., scientifically) with facts and to respect scientific observation and natural law. In the area of science Comte would admit of no freedom of belief. Since all must agree on demonstrated truth, science, he held, provided the one area of knowledge about which there could be no question. This belief is not arbitrary or theocratic, as was the case with Catholicism. Since it is based on observation and demonstration, scientific faith is not imposed, but voluntary, and therefore it need not be enforced by suppressive means. The sciences, then, represented a core of unity—unity of belief.

In order to attain this new unity of belief, Positivism would depend upon an educational system designed to provide opportunity for all. To accomplish this end, Comte envisioned a system like that of Medieval Catholicism with a priesthood dedicated to teaching. Positivist teaching would, like that of the Church, be moral as well as intellectual. The new morality, however, would be based on integrated knowledge (regarding the whole of human nature and environment), on altruism (rather than on the selfish desire for salvation), and on this-world concerns (but "spiritual" rather than material ones). Based on the whole of knowledge and appealing to the whole of human nature (intellect, feelings, and action), the new education and morality would be infinitely superior to any previous system in conducing to the integration both of the individual personality and of the social unit.

In this unified system of beliefs Comte saw little threat to freedom. Certain guarantees of freedom would remain—for example, the right of free inquiry and the right of free speech. Even here some control was to be exercised, for Comte specified that "free inquiry" should always be oriented to man and his welfare. Such prescriptions, however, do raise certain questions about the monitoring process. Who, for example, is in a position to know what is ultimately for the good of man? What kind of power is to be vested in what group to monitor the process of "free inquiry"? Comte provides no reassuring answers on these points. At any rate, Comte felt it necessary to begin with the recasting of public opinion rather than with a program of sociopolitical reforms.

It is, Comte wrote, a "hallucination" and a "disastrous tendency" of the time "to seek in political institutions the solution of all difficulties whatever . . ." (HM, 768). Comte believed, instead, that the reform of institutions could only be the end of the process rather than the starting point. Positivism was to start, first of all, with the reorganization of opinions and the reform of morals. Out of these changes would be born the new political organism.

The realization of the "spiritual power" needed to bring about these changes was, therefore, Comte's first concern. What was needed was an organization like that of the Medieval Church, which had been so effective in welding together diverse peoples. Such an institution would be the ideal vehicle to bring about the Positivist "Republic of the West." Just as Catholicism had transcended national boundaries, the new spiritual power would do so, and the result would be a more solid sense of universal social unity.

Comte's glowing vision of a unified society is outlined for us in the *Course*, but it looks forward to the completed structure of the *Polity*. To those who regard Comte's work as schizophrenically split between science and religion, this sketch should prove instructive. For even in this preliminary overview it is clear that while science may provide the foundations, the raising of the walls of the new society would have to be the work of faith. Comte's conviction that only a "spiritual power" could fuse a society so fragmented and torn as that of his time had long been with him. The detailed program for that reconstructive work appeared some nine years later (in 1851) when the first volume of the *System of Positive Polity* was published.

The *Course in Positive Philosophy* represents Comte's first major step in his program for the reorganization of society. Its systematization of the sciences and its application of scientific method to society were meant to provide the intellectual doctrines which Comte trusted would lead to unity of belief. Needless to say, such unity was not forthcoming. Still, Comte's vast synthesis did not fail to impress readers. Mill, for one, valued Comte's "universal history" as "his greatest achievement, except his review of the sciences, and in some respects more striking even than that." Despite Mill's criticisms of the "social statics" as weak and trite, and despite his objections to certain errors and misjudgments, Mill obviously regarded Comte's "social dynamics" as a landmark in the philosophy of history. What struck Mill, in particular, was the comprehensive scope of Comte's view of history and the richness of his work in suggestive detail.[5] These two features indicate Comte's strengths and at the same time are the clues to inevitable weaknesses as well. For, given this sublunary world with its chaos of mingled purposes and casualties, any reduction to unity is bound to be achieved by a certain arbitrariness in the selection and classification of details. And, perhaps more damaging is the inclusion of a vast deal of nonsensical detail along with perceptive and profound insights. All of these features make Comte's *Course* difficult to summarize, and its contributions to sociology, to historiography, and to philosophy a puzzle to sort out. For our present purposes it seems essential to focus on the dominant patterns of Comtean thought discernible in this major work. These patterns shape themselves around the two key concepts in Comte's thought: order and progress.

While Comte's love of order is both obvious and often commented on, the serious implications of his preoccupation with it need to be mentioned. Comte's predilection for systematizing became more and more obsessive as he went on, and this intensification was reflected in structure and style. What started as a *Course*, a word which designates an educational unit but which also suggests ongoing development, Comte ultimately wanted to call *The System of Positive Philosophy*. This change is significant. In addition, Comte's most-used words direct us toward the process of ordering and systematizing. On every page we encounter words like *organization, reorganization, structure, construction, reconstruction, regulate, regulation, unity, unify, harmonize, harmony*. Comte seems to be fusing intellectual content, structure, and style into an inseparable whole. When, for example, at the end of the *Course* he spoke of the absorption of the aesthetic into the intellectual and social complex of Positivism, that process led him directly into the fusion of nations into harmonious oneness:

While the positive spirit remained in its first phase, the mathematical, it was reproached for its anti-aesthetic tendency: but we see how, when it is systematized from a sociological centre, it becomes the basis of an aesthetic organization no less indispensable than the intellectual and social renovation from which it is inseparable.

The five elements of this great process will each bring their own special contribution to the new system, which will inseparably combine them all. France will bring a philosophical and political superiority; England, an earnest predilection for reality and utility; Germany, a natural aptitude for systematic generalization; Italy, its genius for art; and Spain, its familiar combined sense of personal dignity and universal brotherhood. By their natural cooperation, the positive philosophy will lead us on to a social condition the most conformable to human nature, in which our characteristic qualities will find their most perfect respective confirmation, their completest mutual harmony, and the freest expansion for each and all. (HM, 838)

Having begun the *Course* with a "great fundamental law" regarding the development of the human intelligence (HM, 1), Comte projected therefrom a new society—inevitable, inseparable, and completely harmonious.

A second aspect of the desire for order has to do with the process by which systematizing is made possible. Comte's preoccupation with methodology comes to the fore here. In dealing with each of the sciences, including sociology, Comte (as we have observed) pointed out the development of appropriate methods for dealing with the phenomena concerned.

Perhaps the most slippery concept he dealt with was that of hypothesis. As Comte was aware, hypotheses are fictional constructs, useful in giving direction to scientific investigations so long as they are referred back to reality for proof or disproof (or held as tentative in the expectation of proof). But, as J. S. Mill points out, Comte's résumé at the end of the *Course* curiously extended the use of hypothesis. At this point he was ready to claim the right to adopt "without any vain scruple" hypotheses which could not be proved or disproved, and to do so "in order to satisfy, within proper limits, our just mental inclinations, which always turn, with an instinctive predilection, towards simplicity, continuity, and generality of conceptions, while always respecting the reality of external laws in so far as accessible to us." Comte went on to discuss "the most philosophic point of view" which leads us finally "to conceive the study of natural laws as destined to represent the external world so as to give as much satisfaction to the essential inclinations of our intelligence, as is consistent with the degree of exactitude commanded by the aggregate of our practical wants." Among our "essential inclinations" he cited first of all that "instinctive predilection for order and harmony" which makes us believe any conception, however fictitious, that reduces phenomena to order. Without doubt, our "most eminent mental inclinations" should be satisfied first. But then there certainly remains a considerable area of indeterminateness, in which, Comte continued, it is acceptable to give "direct gratification" to our need of ideality [*besoin d'idéalité*], "by embellishing our scientific thoughts, without injury to their essential reality."[6] In a related passage, Comte warned against those who, examining too minutely some of the established scientific "laws," destroy these hypotheses without being able to supply more satisfactory ones.[7]

Such remarks as these show that Comte's attitude was hardly thoroughly "scientific." From the point of view of someone like Mill, neither our natural "predilection for order and harmony" nor our *besoin d'idéalité* is much of a recommendation for the legitimacy of a hypothesis. Comte's claims represent, for Mill, "a complete dereliction of the essential principles which form the Positive conception of science; and contained the germ of the perversion of his own philosophy" in later years.[8]

Later writers, such as Ducassé and Voegelin, suggest that the appearance of scientific objectivity in the *Course* masked the reality that Comte's life and work were based on just such a fictitious unity as Comte described above. Both insist that the encyclopedic survey of the sciences in the *Course* was never intended to mirror the actual state of the sciences, but that it was the elaboration of an initial intuition—that it was, in fact, the "precipitate of a meditation." As such, the unity projected in the *Course* was anterior to and of an order different from that of the experimental world of science.[9] These readings bring Comte into clearer focus. We can no longer see Comte as just a frustrated mathematician hung up on the ordering of facts and figures, but we need to understand him as a visionary compelled to share his unifying vision and to impose that vision on reality. This reinterpretation of the *Course* certainly brings it much closer to the *Positive Polity* and to the all-encompassing unity that Comte's next work proposed.

But *progress*, as well as *order*, was a key term for Comte. Here, too, we can disengage certain leading ideas and discover through his vision of the orderly progression of past, present, and future Comte's way of reconciling what would seem intrinsically and historically to be opposing forces. Comte believed that minds, individuals, and societies do progress and that they do so in a determinate pattern. While Comte never seemed to probe the cause of this movement, he had, he felt, discerned the pattern. His scrutiny of the past was essential, therefore, because it could show the trajectory of society's progress. This curve would enble us to pinpoint where we are and to calculate where we are headed. But Comte's "history" derives its curve and its unity from the predetermined pattern he imposed on it. The "history" (progress) in the

Course is, in the final analysis, no more oriented to the real world
than its encyclopedia of the sciences; both are projections of Comte's
intuited vision. The apparatus of observed fact, objective method,
and the reference to reality obscure the fictional nature of Comte's
hypothesis: the law of the three stages is inevitable (i.e., "law") only
because Comte acclaimed it as such.

Comte's turning of hypothesis into law determined his analysis
of the present and future as well. Confronted with the chaotic facts
and events of the empirical world, Comte took refuge in mind-
forged system, all the while maintaining that the only reality is the
phenomenal world. Having lost the Christian base which gave meaning to the world of nature, to one's own existence, and to the history
of mankind, Comte found himself in a never-never land where the
very question most important to man was ruthlessly forbidden. But,
as Voegelin observes, to forbid the question is not to abolish it.
Comte's perception of this fact led to his diagnosis of spiritual crisis
and to his creation of a new religion to fill the void: ultimately the
human being is not satisfied to ask How, he wants to know Why.[10]

By the end of the *Course* Comte's diagnosis was complete. At this
point his prescription was still ostensibly within the "laws" of phenomena: what is necessary is a spiritual (moral-intellectual) leadership which will integrate society by unifying its beliefs and
opinions, and a temporal leadership which will organize its production most efficiently. The Why remains implicit—just because
it is a "natural law" immanent in all things to pass through the
theological and transitional stages into the positive stage. It remained for the *System of Positive Polity* to clothe this skeleton with
the vestments of religion.

CHAPTER 4

Positive Polity:
New Wine in Old Bottles

FOR Comte, the weighty volumes in which he set forth the Positive philosophy were not so much an achievement in themselves, but simply the necessary preliminary to his tackling of the great project nearest to his heart—the renovation of society. As we have seen, Comte, from the time of his earliest writings, had talked of a "spiritual power" which might provide mankind with intellectual and moral orientation and which would lead to a new society. Though Comte had, in his youth, "stormed his own Bastilles" (at the Lycée and at the École Polytechnique) in the name of liberty, he had come more and more to see the Revolutionary slogans as only anarchical. Having served their purpose in the destruction of the retrograde system, these slogans had to be supplanted, Comte felt, by a "sound philosophy" that might unify a nation (and with it, a Western world) fragmented into individual groups, each standing on its rights of private judgment and self-governance. To Comte, order in society had become the first necessity, for without order there could be no progress—indeed there could hardly be a society at all. But what could unify a people torn between the progress promised by the revolutionaries and the order offered by the retrograde conservatives? In the *System of Positive Polity* Comte presented his own plan for social reorganization, and that plan was based not simply on a "spiritual power" but on a full-fledged religion.

I *Love Is the Principle: The Religion of Humanity*

By 1848 the *General View of Positivism* had appeared, and even then the new emphasis was apparent. This work, given first in 1847 as a series of lectures, was also to serve later as a general introduction

to the completed *System of Positive Polity* (1854). On the title page
of the *General View* Comte provided a three-part slogan succinctly
pointing the way to Positivism's twin goals, Order and Progress:

> Reorganization, irrespectively of God or king, by the
> worship of Humanity systematically adopted.
> Man's only right is to do his duty.
> The Intellect should always be the servant of the Heart,
> and should never be its slave.

The final version of the motto in the *System of Positive Polity* puts
it more simply:

> The principle, Love;
> The basis, Order;
> The end, Progress.

What strikes a new note in both versions is, of course, the "worship
of Humanity" and the predominance of love as the vital power
coordinating society into a cohesive whole.

As we have noted, the emphasis in the *Positive Philosophy* had
been on the role of science, whose reliance on observed fact and
careful methodology began to provide a basis for consensus of belief.
There were, however, certain problems with which Comte still had
to cope. The first difficulty was that in science itself agreement was
by no means assured. Comte would hardly have admitted this, and
yet he himself, through his practice of *hygiène cérébrale*, lost touch
with or preferred to ignore many of the significant scientific advances
of his time. (Often Comte seems, to our excellent hindsight, pe-
culiarly stubborn in his resistance to the progress of science.) Even
more upsetting to Comte himself was the dispersive effect he saw
in the increasingly specialized studies, which led scientists—the
intellectual leaders—in divergent directions rather than toward
unity. And finally, correct and firm intellectual beliefs were, in
themselves, no guarantee at all that the individual would either
share society's moral views or be motivated by a strong impetus to
moral action. In reality (and despite the faith of a Diderot, for
example, that a science of morals would soon be forthcoming), there
seemed to be an unbridgeable gap between science and morals (or
politics).

Comte, however, felt that the Positive philosophy had begun to
bridge that gulf. His discoveries (of the law of the three states and

the hierarchy of the sciences—that is, of the general laws of sociology) had, for him at least, effected the "complete convergence of the two sets of tendencies, scientific and political, which . . . had divided his attention" (*System*, I, ix).[1] Positivism brought the two realms together in two ways, Comte claimed: since sociology is a science resting upon the other sciences, it absorbs from them materials and methods; since it is, at the same time, a science which makes social questions paramount, it moves science into the domain of human affairs. Nevertheless, even for Comte himself, the synthesis was only complete when he had put this Positive science into its new context as a "sound Philosophy capable of supplying the foundation of true Religion" (*System*, I, xi).

But Comte, not content merely to supply a new context for Positive science, also brought a new method to this work of synthesis. In so doing, he deviated from the purely objective method he had formerly insisted on. The exclusion of feelings from the objective method had been, he came to see, only provisional. Having completed his scientific task, in which "the course of thought was always proceeding from the World in the direction of Man," he now found it essential to include once again the "subjective method as the only source of complete systematisation, the procedure now being from Man outwards toward the World" (*System*, I, xii). Thus the task of the *System of Positive Polity*, its preface promises, would be to place *all* aspects of human nature—that is, feelings, intellect, and action—in their proper relationships. Comte's shift in method was simply his acknowledgment that, after all, mankind needs some guiding principle in the collection and organization of knowledge. Comte believed that the only reasonable reference point had to be the welfare of mankind: only knowledge which is useful to man has true value. Subjective though such a value judgment might be, it provided Comte with the essential footing for his unitary system. While we might have expected, from the early emphasis on intellect, that what Comte aimed at was a religion of science, the end result of his work was, in fact, the development of the Religion of Humanity—a religion based on feelings.

Despite the fact that Comte insisted on the unity of his philosophy and polity (his career is, he tells us, "homogeneous throughout; the end being clearly aimed at from the first" [*System*, I, ix]), he nevertheless devoted a large part of the preface of the *System* to explaining the "apparent changes" in belief and in direction that readers would find in the polity:

Closely connected though they be, these two treatises will therefore exhibit essential differences. Speculative considerations predominate in the first, the object being to show the intellectual superiority of Positivism over all forms of Theology. But in the present treatise, where the moral excellence of true Religion is illustrated, Feeling takes the first place. . . . In the construction of a really complete synthesis, Love is naturally the one universal principle. (*System*, I, xi)

To some of Comte's readers (notably J. S. Mill and Emile Littré, for example, who had supported Comte generously, and who had done so much to make his work known in England and in France), the shift was not "apparent" but real. Many of those who had been attracted by the vast intellectual synthesis of the Positive philosophy could not be induced to accept the equally ambitious construct of the Religion of Humanity. On the other hand, there were many who found in the Religion of Humanity the rescue they had been seeking from the ever-shifting and often desolate seas of unbelief. To clarify the differences between these two areas of Comte's work is to account, at least in part, for the appeal of Positivism to people of almost opposite temperaments and views.

Adding to the confusion, Comte himself talked (with wonder) of the disparities between the "two philosophic lives of such different character," which he had led, each of which had resulted in a crisis and in the creation of a major treatise. As he looked back, his life— or, rather, the mental history of his life—was refracted through the lens of purified vision. What he saw first was the image of a boy torn away too early from the emotional and moral atmosphere of his home. In the light of this new vision, the mother he had found so difficult to get along with in real life became idealized as the embodiment of free-flowing maternal love. His early experiences, together with his unhappy marriage, had, he lamented, stunted his emotional nature:

Withdrawn in early childhood from the ordinary current of home feelings by our disastrous system of public schools, I was artificially urged on to a speculative life for which my nature was but too readily inclined. With manhood came a new and more fatal obstacle to my moral progress from the very course which I had chosen to repair these involuntary shortcomings, the gravity which I already knew. While this deplorable situation lasted (and it was not for me to end it), I was hopelessly cut off from any affection that could satisfy the heart. (*System*, I, xv)

Comte's emotions, long pent up, eventually found in Clotilde de Vaux a dearer object than mother or wife, and his love gushed forth with frightening intensity. Clotilde obviously did not feel the same way about Comte and had difficulty keeping him at arm's length.[2] His passionate entreaties failing, Comte contented himself by transforming the desired mistress into his Beatrice (*System*, I, xvi), his saint (*System*, I, xviii), and his angel of inspiration (*System*, I, xxiv; III, 530; IV, 95–96). While it is easy to be cynical about the facts of this curious relationship, Comte's (often embarrassing) exposure of all the intimate details reveals clearly that this lover saw his private experience as emblematic of the transforming power of love for humanity.

Just as the discovery of the law of the three states had "clicked" to produce in Comte a state of mental and even social unity, the "incomparable year" of his acquaintance with Clotilde translated that unity into the exalted terms of spiritual regeneration. The first intuition had crystallized for him the vision of his work as a whole because it interlocked the sciences with his own personal development and with the sweeping history of civilization through the operation, in all, of a single law. The second intuition, discovered through his love for Clotilde, gave him a much-needed personal experience of love, as well as a concrete emblem for the only integrating, harmonizing force powerful enough to effect the spiritual renovation of humanity. The strong impulsion of that love represented the purest motivating power, while his "union" with Clotilde symbolized the unique way of truly binding individual to family, to society. Love, therefore, is the principle. . . .

The older view of Comte's work as drastically split (the view of Littré and Mill, for example) came in part, then, from Comte's own account of his radically different lives. It came also from the unwillingness of certain "intellectual Positivists" to accept unquestioningly the authority of the self-designated High Priest of Humanity. To them the Religion of Humanity seemed in many ways less acceptable than the Christianity which had become so difficult to believe in. For his part, Littré, calling himself a Positivist still, rejected Comte's polity and pointed to the "subjective method" as a betrayal of Comte's own precepts. (Littré was, of course, also annoyed by Comte's support of Louis Napoleon and by his worship of Clotilde. Such actions, Littré felt, ran counter to Comte's own principles—of freedom and of once-and-for-all commitment to marriage.)

To some followers, too, the extravagancies of Comte's effusions seemed evidence of a return of the mental derangement of 1826. But it seems clear that many Positivists, whatever the reasons they gave, simply could not stomach the strange meld of scientism, Catholicism, and idolatry of Clotilde. They could only mock the elaborate trappings of this new religion which borrowed so much from past religions and yet lacked their vital, supernatural core.

Recent studies of Comte find little evidence of mental derangement or even of a real split in Comte's work. Despite their element of megalomania, Comte's late writings do not show the incoherence of the letters from the period of his breakdown, for example. As for his "Messiah-complex," there have been many sane people who have regarded themselves as having a divine mission. So far as a disjunction in his work is concerned, the "spiritual power" and the system for society's reconstruction were, as Comte kept insisting, part of his plan from the beginning. At most, there was a heightening of the emotional element and an undoubtedly exaggerated emphasis on due reverence for Clotilde. But Comte had been intent from the first on the renovation of society, not on the synthesis of scientific knowledge per se. He was interested in science only for the sake of action.

The projection of a Positivist polity represents, then, both the culmination of Comte's synthesis and something added. Comte's total plan had always been unquestionably grand: he thought to lead not only France, but Western civilization and ultimately the whole world, out of a wasteland marked by hard struggle and bitter conflict into the promised land of Positivist unity. He entered on the next stage of his quest by providing an overview of the new society in the series of lectures given in 1847. These lectures gave the main outline of Comte's plan for systematizing the art of social life—its philosophical base, its social character, its predicted support (the roles of priesthood, women, and the proletariat in this), and its religious dogmas and rituals. This "general view" is the most readable of Comte's works and the best introduction to Positivism for the general reader. As we have already indicated, Comte used this work as the introductory section of the *System of Positive Polity* (1851), whose four volumes present the most complete description of the Religion of Humanity and of the Positivist society.

Another comparatively brief work designed to bring the new religion to the attention of a general audience was the *Positivist Catechism or Summary Exposition of the Universal Religion* (1852). In this series of dialogues between "the priest" and "the lady" (that is, as Comte makes clear, between himself and Clotilde) the main aspects of the Religion of Humanity are explained. The relatively loose dialogue form hardened, in this work, into the exposition of a fixed dogma. Given the vastness and complexity of Comte's philosophy and polity, we can easily see the wisdom of the "general view" and of a "summary exposition." At any rate, these shorter works show that Comte was aware that if he wished to reach a wide audience he must make his ideas as accessible as possible.

The last of Comte's major works, the *Subjective Synthesis*, is, on the other hand, an exposition of the new doctrines directed to an entirely different audience. In this curious work Comte, writing in 1856, imagined himself as addressing the teachers of Positivism when this movement should have become well established, that is, in 1927. In the first volume of the *Synthesis* (the only one of the projected four volumes completed) Comte began an exposition of mathematics and logic designed to help the educators of the future deal with the basic sciences using the new approach, the subjective synthesis.

Taken all together, the *System of Positive Polity* (1854), the *Positivist Catechism* (1852), and the *Subjective Synthesis* (1856) spell out for us in endless (and sometimes ridiculous) detail Positivism's sociological and educational base, its religious dogmas and worship, and its social and political structure. The final section of the *System* even projects Revelation-like into the future to envision and to program the establishment of Positivism on earth.

Comte's plan for the reconstitution of society is laid out most fully in the *System of Positive Polity*. This awesome work overwhelms the reader by its comprehensiveness in scope, by its rigorous organization of all of life, and by its attention to minutiae. But this all-embracing systematization chills the reader, too, with its stultifying detail and with its frightening totalitarian potential. For Positivism, despite Comte's insistence on the voluntary nature of the intellectual and emotional consent it requires, becomes ultimately a lesson in duty and submission. The main instrument for teaching this submission was the new religion Comte had devised.

Unquestionably, then, the most important part of this treatise, the *System*, is that which deals with the Religion of Humanity. The new religion, based on the subjective principle of love, was the great foundation on which Comte proposed to reconstruct society.

For Comte, himself, the return to subjective principle and method was not in conflict with the objective method so dear to him as scientist. By use of the "subjective," Comte meant merely to recognize that Intellect (or Science) stands in need of some guiding principle in its selection of the proper questions and goals for mankind. Once that guidance is given, scientific method finds its appropriate function, which is to determine by rigorous, objective analysis the most effective means of achieving the indicated goal. In Positivism, love-as-the-principle would channel scientific effort into the kinds of inquiry useful to mankind in achieving its "proper goal," which is the harmonious integration, personal and social, of order and progress.

Like the Utilitarians, then, Comte determined value by the standard of usefulness even though he rejected their materialism (their measuring of value solely in terms of economic well-being) and their encouragement of the egoistic instincts (their attempt to build a social theory on a psychological base of self-interest). Usefulness is, however, as problematical in the context of Positivism as it is in that of Utilitarianism. Who is to determine what is useful or how useful an activity or institution is? How immediate do useful results have to be? Many of the inquiries, for example, which led to great advances for humanity (even in Comte's own view of its history) would not have struck anyone as particularly useful at the time they were undertaken. What is useful to the harmonious development of society seems not to have been, for Comte at least, open to question. His system simply provided a final authority, a priesthood, and ultimately a High Priest (himself, of course), who would, without any hesitation, tell people what the proper questions and activities were. But whatever we may think of Comte's goals and standards, he at least tried to bring into the open the problem of values—a problem which has only grown more acute since his time and which too often lies unacknowledged behind decisions regarding such things as scientific research, educational priorities, and governmental budgets. Comte's criterion of usefulness led him to look with Swiftian contempt (with none of Swift's sardonic wit, however) on much of the scientific activity of his day. What was useful, Comte claimed, boiled down to what increased our power over nature so that humankind might live more humanly—better adjusted to environment and more in harmony with fellow humans.

With social unity as the goal dictated by love, the practical problem was to find the means to accomplish this goal. Comte's analysis of human nature led him to believe that social tensions arise because the egoistic feelings in each of us (the nutritive, sexual, and maternal instincts, and pride and vanity, for example) naturally outweigh the social (or altruistic) feelings. Social disunity is then seen as a moral problem, and consequently there is no hope of solving it through political action, institutional reform, or redistribution of wealth. Only as the altruistic feelings could be cultivated to the point where they would predominate over the selfish interests of the individual could society flourish.

Comte's political program was, therefore, inseparable from moral reform, and both are based on the imperative need to modify egoism by the combined influence of family and religion. The work of religion is then cut out for it: "the grand object of religion being to teach us to live for others, it must essentially consist in regulating the direct cultivation of our sympathetic instincts" (*System*, IV, 77). Comte's definition of religion is somewhat offbeat in that it centers not on the supernatural, but on religion's power to unify: religion, he wrote, expresses "that state of complete harmony peculiar to human life, in its collective as well as in its individual form, when all the parts of Life are ordered in their natural relations to each other" (*System*, II, 8). By "all parts," Comte meant the "three kinds of phenomena of which our life consists, Thoughts, Feelings, and Actions" (*System*, I, 6). To establish this "state of complete unity," he continued, "its task must consist both in *regulating* each personal life, no less than in *combining* different individual lives" (*System*, II, 8; italics his). Since the theologies of the past failed mainly because they did not satisfy the intellect, Comte saw no recourse but to create a new religion to fulfill *all* these functions.

While Comte would never have said "God is dead" (for that would be to admit that He had once lived), the old religions certainly appeared to him to be defunct. In an age of science, mankind could hardly be expected to believe in imaginary supernatural beings. An acceptable religion would, Comte postulated, need a Being to worship who was convincingly real and yet not limited to today's concept of morality. In addition, the dogmas of the new church would have to be based on reality and developed with logical consistency. Comte set out systematically to fill these needs. Yet even as he was molding religion anew, Comte took his institutional model from the past—from the Medieval Church, whose establishment of a vital spiritual power seemed to him the greatest socializing force in the history of mankind.

II *Reverencing Humanity: A New God*

In order for the new religion to restore the sense of meaning and direction provided by Medieval Catholicism, it needed first of all to find a substitute for the grand but outmoded concept of God. Discarding all of the "fictitious gods" of antiquity, Comte proposed that mankind worship a new entity, the Great Being of Humanity, that is, "the whole constituted by the beings, past, future, and present, which cooperate willingly in perfecting the order of the world" (*System*, IV, 27). Such a Great Being, says Comte, is real and therefore acceptable to the scientist, who deals only with observable fact. This Great Being is also "relative" and therefore modifiable as mankind's ideas of perfection develop.

Comte recognized no rival gods. Despite his borrowings from Catholicism and his interest in certain Christian saints and writers (St. Paul, Dante, and Thomas à Kempis, for example), Comte scarcely mentioned Jesus except for fleeting references to the "fiction of Christ." In his description of Jesus and Mary in the *Course of Positive Philosophy* (HM, 626), Comte presented both figures as if they were "ideal models" constructed by the Catholic Church. It seems that while Comte was willing to set up shop in the company of prophets and disciples of other gods, a transcendental god made flesh would have been unfair competition for what Eric Voegelin calls the "immanent, sociological God" of Auguste Comte.[3]

In Comte's view, Christianity needed to be replaced not only because belief in a supernatural god had become impossible, but also because its main goal, personal salvation, reinforced egoistic rather than social instincts. By focusing worship on Humanity itself, Comte expected the Positivist religion to turn this process around. And furthermore, by limiting the worship to those who "cooperate willingly" in perfecting the unity of Humanity, Comte fixed attention on the feelings and activities which foster a sense of the corporate body.

In addition to these advantages, Comte claimed that the concept of the Great Being would free religion of all the intellectual difficulties attaching to the idea of a supernatural Being. The defenders of the Positivist faith would find, for example, that traditional arguments for the existence of God had become irrelevant. And, perhaps best of all, Positivists would have no need to concern themselves with the sticky problem of accounting for the existence of evil in a world created by a God both good and omnipotent.

All in all, Comte believed that the Religion of Humanity could satisfy both intellect and heart. The Great Being would provide a unifying focus of belief, and it would encourage social cooperation by making the integrated society itself the object of worship.

The elimination of God from his religion left Comte with what T. H. Huxley dubbed "Catholicism minus Christianity." Such a summary dismissal fails, however, to do justice to the system Comte was in the process of creating. Having stressed the value of Medieval Christianity's contributions to societal development, Comte naturally enough borrowed the Church's techniques for inculcating its teachings and for cultivating a mystical sense of unity. To achieve these same ends, Comte incorporated into the Positivist religion as many of the familiar forms and practices as he could.

III *Cultivating Saintliness: A New Worship*

In setting up his elaborate system of devotions and commemorations, Comte seems to have succumbed once and for all to the influence of Catholicism. The spiritual exercises Comte prescribed for Positivists required an almost monastic devotion: there were specific rituals (private, domestic, and public) for particular times of day, for the regular worship services, and for special occasions.

Since the focal figure, God, was missing from these devotions, Comte centered Positivist worship on the heroes of the past and on womankind—special (or "concrete") representatives of the Great Being. The great heroes of the past were those who symbolize the progress of mankind: each represented a significant step forward in knowledge, or in moral perception, or in social organization. As for the worship of woman, it was designed to make real the abstract love of humanity by embodying it in its purest form. Comte's premise was that in their three roles (as mother, wife, and daughter) women bring out in men the three essential forms of social feeling— veneration, attachment, and benevolence (kindness and concern for the future). Hence the worship of woman was to prepare man for the worship of Humanity, past, present, and future. The ideal figure of woman was no longer to be the Virgin Mary. Comte chose to replace her with three women who would represent the threefold aspects of womanhood: Rosalie Boyer (Comte's mother), Clotilde de Vaux (Comte's spiritual wife and the new "virgin-mother"), and

Sophie Bliaux (the "adopted daughter," who looked after Comte).
And, of course, the greatest of these was Clotilde.

To formalize Positivist religion, Comte appropriated many a device from Catholicism and from its Revolutionary supplanters. There
was, for example, the Positivist catechism. There was also a new
calendar, complete with a roll of Positivist saints to take the place
of traditional (or revolutionary) ones. In working out his calendar,
Comte's systematizing mind adopted a neatly regular thirteen-
month calendar, in which each month was to be devoted to com-
memorating a certain kind of contribution to civilization's progress.
Comte's calendar set aside special days for ceremonies honoring
individuals whose contributions to Humanity had been outstanding,
and for festivals celebrating the most significant dates in mankind's
history. A glance at the Positivist Calendar suffices to show the
systematizing and synthesizing nature of Comte's work. There
Moses, Confucius, and Mahomet share honors with Galileo, Newton, Lavoisier, and Gall. Thus the Positivist Calendar traces out the
progress of mankind even as it invites the worship of the exemplary
heroes of the past. (Jesus, however, does not appear in this register
of saints.)

The most sacred manifestation of Positivist worship was in its
formal sacraments, another borrowing from Catholicism. In the
Religion of Humanity there were normally to be nine of these rites:
presentation, initiation, admission, destination, marriage, maturity,
retirement, transformation, and incorporation. However, since the
rites of destination, maturity, and retirement have to do with a
professional career, they would normally be omitted in the case of
women, whose lives were, as a rule, to be domestic (*System*, IV,
109). For all individuals these sacraments were to mark the significant stages in a human life from its commencement to its enshrine-
ment after death in the hallowed body of the Great Being. By these
rites the individual would be enfolded, as it were, in successive
reminders of his or her responsibility to make humanity more human. Only by fulfilling that responsibility could the individual become a member of the Great Being. And only when a life was over
could it be evaluated as having indeed cooperated in the perfection
of humanity and as having therefore merited incorporation in the
Great Being.

Stripped of the "busy work" designed to inculcate and to reinforce
habits of altruistic thought and action, the emotional core of the
Religion of Humanity can be seen. Comte wanted, first of all, to

give modern "scientific" man something beyond himself to worship. And so Comte created the Great Being of Humanity—a god transcending the self, but not supernatural. Comte wanted, in the second place, to provide mankind with a new goal to substitute for the salvation-in-the-other-world which had come to seem chimerical. For this Comte created "subjective immortality"—a new kind of immortality, in which the individual, having cooperated in the perfecting of humanity, lives on in the memories of other people. The daily acts of worship thus *are* the immortality each human being craves. Comte's religion was designed, then, to fulfill the emotional needs of the individual by giving his life enhanced value and unifying purpose. And, because Positivism made the good of humanity central to the individual's well-being and immortality, Comte believed that his religion guaranteed social unity as well.

IV   *Satisfying the Intellect: The New Dogma*

While the Great Being provided the emotional center for worship, this need was obviously not the only one a modern religion had to meet. The intellect had to be satisfied as well as the heart. Consequently, Comte took great pains to show the empirical and logical soundness of Positivist doctrine.

The intellectual core of Positivist religion is found in the series of fifteen "laws," outlined by Comte in the fourth volume of the *System of Positive Polity* (pp. 154–60). This codification demonstrates the synthesis of objective and subjective laws attained by sociology. The goal of Positivist education is to bring the individual to an understanding of these laws, which pertain to the physical world, to mankind, and to society—in a word, to the whole hierarchy of being.

While we may find it difficult to adjust to the idea of a Credo beginning with "I believe in forming the simplest hypothesis; I believe in the invariability of nature's laws . . . ," Comte was simply, in a Cartesian and Church-Father mode, formulating what he felt he (i.e., mankind) could affirm with certainty regarding the activities of the human mind. Just as Comte's index of progress was the history of the human mind, sociology was, for him, the ultimate science of the human mind—the sum total of its activities and productions throughout history and in society. Such knowledge was the only satisfactory intellectual basis for the kind of religion Comte envisioned. Thus sociology itself provided the requisite synthesis—

the coordination of objective and subjective methods and of all knowledge—to unify mankind's beliefs and goals.

Comte believed that his own coordination of feelings and intellect would meet the basic needs of humanity for just such unity. For one thing, Positivist religion did away with the hostility between science and religion by making science central to religion. In addition, Comte's religion resolved the difficulty inherent in most religions whose central dogmas, or fixed body of beliefs, were incompatible with progress. Progress was built into the Religion of Humanity insofar as both order (the invariability of natural laws) and progress (the possiblity of modification of phenomena with certain limits) were part of Positivist dogma. Progress was further incorporated into this religion in the notion of Humanity Comte asked Positivists to worship. What they were expected to love was the best that man could possibly be or accomplish, and that *best* could, of course, always be redefined as humanity's moral sense becomes refined. Whoever invented the term *meliorism*, Comte clearly believed in the concept.

Even the invention of a religion designed to ennoble and to socialize humankind was not an end in itself for Comte, however. The Religion of Humanity was to provide the foundation (the dogma) and the heart (the unifying power) of the Positivist state which Comte believed was about to come into being.

V Order Is the Basis: The Sociocracy

The transformed society Comte envisioned was one in which the practical power of might and money would be offset by the vital strength of the new spiritual power. Furthermore, this realignment could be brought about, Comte claimed, without a radical wiping out of existing political institutions and industrial organizations. While both aims seem admirable enough when presented in general terms, the filled-in outline is another matter. We need to see how Comte's vision of a "spiritually renewed" society hardened into a rigidly unified structure prescribed and monitored throughout.

Comte found his model for the new social organization in the family unit. The society he projected was therefore hierarchical: each segment of this society, like each family member, would have a well-defined role to play in its proper sphere of influence—a role related to the "member's" natural strengths, whether these might be in the field of intellect, of emotions, or of action. But just as the family has a kind of double hierarchy depending on whether we are looking to the mother (superior in affections and morals) or to the father (superior in intellect and action), so, too, in the larger society. There the separation of powers would result in a double hierarchy with *spiritual* leadership in the hands of a Positivist priesthood and *temporal* authority exercised by the captains of industry, a new patriciate controlling both government and industry. The proposed new order might be schematized as shown in Table 1. While a double hierarchy would seem to have serious built-in tensions, Comte presented his plan as one which would secure unity because it would reward both spiritual and temporal merit, and also because it would satisfy society's basic need for both order and progress.

Since the spiritual power was the instrument by which Comte hoped to effect social change, he focused most of his attention on the agents of this new power—priests, proletariat, and women. Nevertheless, Comte did expect drastic changes to occur eventually in the realms of politics and industry; for, although he was a realist when it came to acknowledging the power of might and money in determining the temporal order, Comte also believed that such power could be tempered by an organized effort to cultivate the social instincts and to enforce responsible leadership through the pressure of public opinion. Obviously, however, it was going to take a militant spiritual force to change the direction of both cumbersome bureaucracy and ruthless capitalism. The spiritual power of Positivism had its work cut out for it, indeed.

VI   *Reorganizing Opinion: The Spiritual Power*

Believing that the peculiar strength of Catholicism had derived from its separation of spiritual from temporal power, Comte wanted to entrust spiritual (i.e., moral and intellectual) leadership to a priesthood whose purity would be safeguarded by virtue of its having neither wealth nor political power. Priests were to be excluded from all political and practical occupations in order to guarantee their disinterestedness and to keep their minds free from preoccupation. Their support was therefore to be provided by the state. Under such circumstances priestly authority could rest only on persuasion, not on force. What Comte envisioned, then, was not a society ruled by a philosopher-king, but one in which the philosopher-priest would exercise a guiding influence on the religious, intellectual, and practical life of the community.

TABLE 1

Spiritual — Power base: moral influence (force of numbers and of public opinion)		Temporal — Power base: wealth	
Sphere of Influence	Function		Function
High Priest / *Priests*		**Triumvirate of Bankers** / *Patriciate**	
Intellect: Sociology* replacement of military-theological by industrial-scientific order	priestly functions, scientific research and synthesis, education (intellectual), counsel in public and private matters, classification of society	Leaders in: banking, commerce, manufacturing, agriculture,	organization and management of the industrial complex
Women			
Affects: Sociolatry* replacement of theology by the Religion of Humanity	education (affective, moral), moral influence within the family, moral influence through "salons"	[Middle classes—to be absorbed into the ranks of management or of the proletariat]	
Proletariat*		*Proletariat*	
Action: Sociocracy* replacement of the military by the industrial order	moral influence through public opinion, moral influence through clubs and pubs		real production of material goods

(Although they are not included in this table, even the animals which have contributed to civilization are included in Comte's chain of social beings.)
*Indicates Comte's own terminology.

The religious duties of the priests were to include such predictable tasks as preaching, performing religious ceremonies, and administering the sacraments. These spiritual leaders were also to advise the other members of society and to admonish those who might violate the moral law. Should private reprimand prove ineffective, the priests might then resort to the stricter measure of public remonstrance. In extreme cases excommunication might be necessary. These various means, if backed by public opinion, would be effective weapons, Comte felt, in the enforcement of moral law.

In the intellectual realm, the role of the clergy would be to carry on scientific and philosophic studies. The priests' own encyclopedic education was designed to prepare them for their "principal function," which would be to complete (or "coordinate") Positive knowledge and to cast it into a viable educational program. Formal (intellectual) education was to be in the hands of the priests. Their task would be to develop the intellect without undercutting the early lesson (taught by the mother) that the heart must be supreme. In order to avoid narrow specialization each professor would be "bound to teach in succession the seven fundamental sciences" (*System*, IV, 233). Thus each teacher would shepherd two classes, one male and one female (the sexes separate but equal—at least in education) through the seven-year program, whereupon the priest would begin the cycle anew with two new groups of students. At all points these teachers must guard against "intellectualism" by stressing the submission of the intellect to feeling. The encyclopedic education must reinforce this lesson by always demonstrating the links between the external world and human bodies and human souls. Needless to say, Comte saw the priesthood as a consecrated vocation which would require the highest moral and intellectual qualities as well as the utmost dedication to education.

The same intellectual and moral capabilities were also essential if the priests were to play a significant role in the practical world. While priests were not to be directly involved in the grubby world of business and politics, they were still to be a major force modifying and directing the energies of society's leaders. In this area, the priests' part would be to give moral guidance regarding important public and private actions, and to arbitrate conflicts (*System*, I, 34). The clergy's most powerful weapon here, Comte felt, would be the active support of public opinion. Priests could also fall back on public remonstrance and excommunication should their advice be ignored and society's good be threatened. In sum, the role of the priesthood envisioned by Comte would be educative and consultative.

At the head of the priestly hierarchy, there was to be a High Priest—a Positivist Pope, so to speak. Comte naturally saw himself in this role and began to carry out the appropriate duties in the Positivist Society, which had been formed in 1848. By 1850 Comte had conferred "the three chief social sacraments, those connected with birth, marriage, and death" (*System*, I, xxv). And, as successive volumes of the *System of Positive Polity* appeared, Comte made use of the prefaces to communicate to his flocks and to report on the progress of various Positivist missions—in the provinces, in Holland, in England, and in America. Comte's playing of the High Priestly role accounts also for the letters in which he proposed alliances with the Jesuits, with Czar Nicholas, and with the Grand Vizier Reschid-Pacha.[4] By the 1850's Comte's imagination had reached far beyond the Republic of the West to seek alliances with Russia and the Islamic world.

As Comte became more confident in his role as High Priest, the totalitarian tendencies of Positivism surfaced more and more. The arbitrary control Comte exercised—or at least tried to exercise— over the thought and daily life of his disciples makes us conscious that order and regulation can mean simply systematizing (regularizing), or they can mean giving orders (or regulating). Comte himself commented on the double meaning. Needless to say, Comte did not see his priestly injunctions as arbitrary. He insisted always that the Positivist Church was to be a fellowship of those *willing to submit* to the direction of the High Priest and his assistants: moral order was to be achieved through the voluntary submission of the individual to his intellectual and moral superiors, the priests.

Despite the strong leadership to be expected from the priesthood, Comte well knew that such a group could not by itself transform society. He also knew that neither the industrial leaders nor the middle classes were likely to help much in the reconstructive process. The captains of industry, busy expanding their empires, were no doubt useful to society, but their attention seemed to be fixed more on increasing profits, rather than on ensuring that those gains would alleviate the misery of the poor workers. As for the second group, the middle classes, they were in Comte's eyes the worst of parasites, motivated only by greed and self-interest. Comte regarded this bourgeoisie as destined to disappear as its members became absorbed either into the ranks of management or of the workers (*System*, IV, 406). Expecting no assistance from either the industrial leaders or the middle class, Comte depended on the backing of women and of the proletariat to bring about the reign of Positivism. In these two groups at least, Comte felt, the social feelings were strong, and therefore he looked to them for support.

Women, in particular, were to have a grand role in the establishment of Positivism. Even so, Comte's own "retrograde" tendencies are much in evidence in his placing of women, for, despite the worship of women, Comte would relegate real women to a purely domestic role. Comte based this judgment on his rather cliché reading of woman's nature as one in which feelings are preeminent. Since women are more emotional than men, Comte claimed, their proper sphere of influence is within the family—as tender companions to men and as "pure" procreators of future generations.

Indeed, precisely because the social feelings are stronger in women than in men, women represent moral superiority and are, therefore, worthy of veneration. In a Utopia ruled by love, women would be supreme.[5] But, Comte added, real life is full of difficulties which require other powers: energy, strength, intellect, talent. Since "in all kinds of force, whether physical, intellectual, or practical, it is certain that Man surpasses Woman, in accordance with the general law prevailing throughout the animal kingdom," man's power or force must rule in the world of action (*System*, I, 169). Generally, therefore, women were to have no political or industrial power, for feeling's proper function is to act as a modifier of practical energy.[6]

Though they normally would have no public role, then, women would still have great moral and social influence in the Positivist society. Within the family they were to give their children moral guidance, to educate the young in art and poetry, and to remonstrate (gently, of course) with those who might deviate from their duty. Their influence would radiate out from the home through the *salons*, in which they would play an active role. These new *salons*, replacing those of the elite aristocracy, would provide a gracious milieu for the discussion of ideas.

All of this domesticity means, of course, that women would have to be provided for. It is a "natural law of the human race," Comte averred, "that Man should provide for Woman" (*System*, I, 199–200). In marriage this provision would continue to be a voluntary personal obligation, but in cases where a woman has no father or husband, maintenance should be guaranteed by society just as it would be for the priesthood.

Marriage was to be regarded as a sacred attachment in the Positivist system. While this union has its origin in (selfish) sexual instinct, the conjugal relationship is refined by the purity of woman's love. Out of the personal experience of strong love, Comte maintained, "we rise by degrees to sincere affection to all mankind" (*System*, I, 189). Comte regarded this experience as so important to the development of the social nature that he stipulated that Positivist priests (unlike their Catholic counterparts) be married. Comte's prescriptions regarding marriage were based, then, on its importance not simply to the individual, but to society at large. As ever, Comte stressed moral duty rather than individual rights. In the Positivist order, marriage was to be an exclusive union. Indissoluble, not legally but morally, marriage also carried with it the sacred moral duty of perpetual widowhood. In other words, where sexual instinct was, there let moral commitment be.

In defining marriage and in prescribing woman's role, Comte was far from sympathetic to the main ideas of woman's liberation movements. Though he advocated equality in the education of boys and girls, he regarded equality of the two sexes as "contrary to their nature." The two sexes naturally tend, he insisted, to become more and more differentiated. And further, "the direction, then, of progress in the social condition of woman is this: to render her life more and more domestic" (*System*, I, 198, 200). From Comte's point of view, these "natural laws" indicated the proper role for women. In addition, he regarded the moral superiority of women as the direct result of their being apart from the competitiveness of the market place. Working women would only become tainted by the aggressiveness and self-seeking of the work-a-day world. The competitive spirit fostered in that world would also tend to corrupt with rivalry the relationship between man and woman. Comte saw the business world as hostile precisely to the sympathetic feelings he felt were women's greatest asset. The role of woman was thus to be based upon "the constitution of her nature" as the "spontaneous organ of feeling" (*System*, I, 204); for happiness for her, as for everyone, could come only with the fulfillment of her nature.

The worship of woman proposed by Comte was a celebration of this all-important human element, feeling—that is, man was to worship in woman that which unites humanity in all times and all places. The ideal society that Comte strove for was that represented by Chivalry, an order built around the worship of woman. The knight, inspired by pure affection, dedicated himself to his lady's service, and from this commitment there developed a voluntary combination of the strong for the protection of the weak. Comte wanted exactly this kind of unity in his new society and saw no reason why Chivalry, freed from the limitations placed on it by Catholicism, should not come to glorious life again in Positivism. Chivalry's elements—the motivation from within (love), the commitment to service, the steadfastness of purpose, the dedication to needy Humanity—satisfied an "essential want of society." And, Comte added, "It would be strange indeed for a system like Positivism, the main object of which is to strengthen the social spirit, not to appropriate the institution [Chivalry] which is the noblest product of that spirit" (*System*, I, 206).

We are turned back to Clotilde and to the sacred altar (the famous red chair on which she sat) as to a magnet. And we perceive that women are profoundly important to the realization of the Comtean program not simply because they are the focus of man's feelings, but because man's relationship with them symbolizes the process of integration: instinct, passion, purification. The worship of woman was to begin a new order of Chivalry—a firm and beautiful construct built on the shifty and primitive urges of sexual attraction. Comte even projected a future state in this construct—the purified utopia of the Virgin Mother (*System*, IV, 60; 212–13).

The Positivist sociocracy, however, did not depend upon women's reaching that degree of purity. Comte refused to allow that he was projecting a utopia at all. He felt that he was simply describing the next step in civilization's progress—a step that was prepared for and inevitable. And he invited women and workingmen to share in the great task of reconstruction.

The workers, too, were destined to play a major role in the establishment of Positivism. Indeed, Comte emphasized not only that the proletariat was the principal productive base of the new society, but also that the sole way of realizing the new system was for the philosopher-priest to enter into alliance with the working people (*System*, I, 110).[7]

The proletariat was of particular concern to Comte because he, like other social theorists of his time, was aware that the needs of the working people were most pressing. Despite their contribution to production, the workers continued to live in poverty and uncertainty. The doctrine of "sovereignty of the people," which revolutionaries had thought would solve the problems of the poor, had not proved, in reality, to be an effective way of bettering the worker's lot. Hence Comte dismissed this doctrine as raising a false issue: treating the matter as a political issue simply engaged people in "useless discussions about the distribution of power, instead of fixing their attention on the manner in which it is used" (*System*, I, 154). The real issues, Comte claimed, were social and moral rather than political. For similar reasons, Comte disagreed with Socialist and Communist programs. While he did agree with the Socialists and Communists regarding the social nature of property, Comte accepted neither the "criticism and inaction" of socialism nor the political-legal actions of communism. Communism's aims—to suppress individuality and to remove the leaders of industry—went, to Comte's mind, against the grain of the "true laws of society" (*System*, I, 126–27). The Positivist ideal was that property should be controlled by moral, not legal (or governmental), agencies (*System*, I, 131; IV, 412–13).

Thus Comte, while recognizing the urgency of the workers' needs, proposed that the only way of effecting real and lasting reform was through the modification of public opinion—that is, through what would seem to be a long, slow process. To get all the forces in society to work for the common good, Comte insisted that it was necessary first to establish what the common good requires, then to create the conditions necessary to bring about this goal. The achievement of reform, then, depended not only on a recognized code of principles, but on an adequate education and the "healthy direction" of public opinion. Since Comte believed that he had himself provided the "code of principles," his interest in education is understandable: he saw it as the only instrument capable of bringing about essential changes in society.

Comte's lifelong concern for and appeal to the workers were based on his desire to effect specific changes in their condition through education. Throughout his life he made deliberate efforts to recruit into his courses working people, whose character seemed to him especially open to the influence of Positivism. He perceived in this class a strong sense of the real and useful, as well as an unusual generosity of feeling. The workers' lives, he felt, reflected little of the concern for the material gain and worldly success that vitiated the life of the middle class. The laborers, whose work demanded little in the way of responsibility and intellectual effort, would also have more time and more freedom of mind to absorb Positivist teaching. In addition, Comte felt that the life of the workers tended to develop the social instincts, in the form of home affections, social sympathy, and respect for superiors. Less dominated than their more successful "superiors" by the egoistic drives (of ambition, avarice, and vanity), the working people could, Comte believed, be educated to help create and unified to help exert the strong moral force necessary to regenerate society.

The educational program that Comte outlined was designed for just this purpose. In fact, the main task of Positivism was to make education available generally, especially to those like women and working folk who had had little opportunity to enjoy this advantage. Though Comte often sounds condescending regarding the intellectual capacities of women and workers, he obviously thought them capable of understanding the courses in mathematics, astronomy, and sociology he had, for so many years, been offering free to the general public.

But, in additon to extending the advantages of education, Comte also wanted to make Positivist education different from that of the traditional system. Conventional education, based essentially on training in rhetoric, developed neither real intellectual power nor social solidarity, said Comte, but turned out "mere literary men and lawyers." Even though the alternative schools (like l'École Polytechnique) were turning out men of science, these schools forced the kind of specialization which produced "thoroughly narrow" minds (*System*, I, 150, 152). Positivist education was to remedy these radical defects—it was to cultivate both the intellect and the moral (i.e., social) nature.

In drawing up his own educational system, Comte relied once again on his law of the three stages. Believing that the individual, like society, passes through each of these stages in turn, Comte geared his program to them. Thus, in the early years spent under the influence of mother and home, the child's education should be spontaneous rather than formal. The mother should develop the child's feelings for poetry, music, the visual arts, and language. This "theological stage" should be a period in which the child's emotional nature and powers of observation freely develop.

From about the age of seven to fourteen, education would be more systematic, and it would be organized to develop the child's knowledge of the fine arts—poetry, music, and drawing. At this level, the student would be expected to learn the principal Western languages. This kind of study should not be by formal lecture, but by practicing the art, Comte said, more or less systematically. These languages would serve to cultivate the child's sense of community, even though all this while the child remains within the family. At this stage, the child would become familiar with the literary masterpieces in these languages.

At about the age of fourteen, the child would begin the next stage, seven years of formal education. This course of study would consist of a series of public lectures explaining the general laws of the various orders of phenomena, the coordination of all these laws, and their relationship to the social purpose. Following Comte's general classification scheme, the teacher would devote a year to the study of each science, beginning with mathematics and passing then to the inorganic and organic sciences. The final two years, devoted to sociology and to moral science, would complete the child's general education. The inclusion of "moral science" at the end is a notable addition to the program outlined in the *Course*. For gifted students a more specialized professional education would be devised or added on.

Comte's educational system was designed to offer certain advantages over other systems. For one thing, it left the child at home where the socializing influence of mother and family could, he felt, work most effectively. The program was also meant to create a more open world, where brains and talent might be recognized. In aspiring to convey something more than specialized knowledge or ingenuity in the manipulation of language, Comte wanted not only to give each child breadth of knowledge, but also to cultivate clearsightedness, consistency, and wisdom—that is, what he sought was education in its truest sense (*System*, I, 152).

And finally, such an education, cultivating both mental powers and social feelings, would also create a unified proletariat. Combining unity (moral and intellectual) of public opinion with the strength of numbers, the people would be able to exert the moral force necessary to curb selfish greed and ambition. Making education freely accessible was the first step in the implementation of Comte's plan to organize the workers and thus the beginning of the reorganization of society.

VII   *Reorganizing Society: The Temporal Order*

However much Comte directed attention away from political and social institutions, his proposed Republic of the West was to be radically different from the order familiar to nineteenth-century Frenchmen. Reform of these institutions was, however, to be the end-product of a natural and gradual process rather than its beginning. But, in the long run, as the spiritual power of Positivism exerted its influence, Comte was convinced that it would create a new political order, organize scientific-industrial development, and restructure society.

In the political field, as we have already seen, Comte watched with dismay the confusion of the times and the violent oscillations between dictatorship and representative government. Though Comte believed these problems would only be really solved when the state achieved its definitive (i.e., Positive) form, he felt that France had already begun the transition to Positivism with the establishment of the dictatorship of Louis Napoleon in 1851. The direction of events seemed so promising to Positivism that Comte undertook to describe the various stages of the transitionary period and to predict its completion within thirty-three years (*System*, IV, 387). Comte's philosphy was, in fact, the nineteenth century's *Leviathan* insofar as it justified strong, centralized government. Indeed, Comte's ideal rulers tended to be "enlightened despots"—men like Frederick the Great or the Czar of Russia, who kept the prerogatives of absolute power but promoted certain reforms.[8] Comte expected his philosophy to appeal to just such leaders, and through them he hoped to gain the position which would give Positivism official sanction. Comte's sanguine expectation was that within seven years he would be appointed Director of Education, whereupon he would put into effect the Positivist program of education. With that appointment the second phase of the transition would begin. The prestige and power connected with this position would strengthen Positivism, in addition to providing Comte with the means of propagandizing (and conditioning?) students on an unprecedented scale. Within another five years, Comte believed, France would be ready for the next stage, this one to be marked by a political change—the passing of power into the hands of a Positivist triumvirate. Thus Positivism, working through education and religion to change opinions and morals, would gradually demonstrate its superiority to other systems and prepare for the new kind of state. Within twenty-one more years, Comte calculated, Positivism would gain ascendancy—the whole process having taken some thirty-three years.

While Comte did not believe he could convert all of France to Positivism within this time, he did think that Positivism could rally to its cause a substantial number of leaders—enough, at any rate, to provide the nation with the unity and direction it needed. That leadership would bring into being the Republic of the West with Paris as the rightful center—not only of France, but ultimately of the world. As a unit this Republic would be governed in its temporal concerns by a triumvirate of bankers and in its spiritual concerns by the High Priest (and his advisors). Their power would be that of a dictatorship, for none of these authorities were to be elected: once these posts were created and filled, the holder of the position would select his successor. The only curbing of the state's power would be in the guarantee of certain liberties: the freedom of the general public would be safeguarded by ensuring the rights of free speech, of free press, and of voluntary association. (Comte never seemed to notice how rarely dictatorships guarantee such rights.) The moral admonitions of the priests (supported by public opinion) Comte also regarded as an effective way of moderating temporal power within the Republic.

The Republic of the West projected by Comte was to be an international entity created out of diversity. Existing nations would break up naturally, he believed, into a number of small republics, each carefully limited as to size and population. France itself, for example, would be divided into seventeen republics, each ruled by a triumvirate of bankers (just like the larger Republic). The West would be divided into seventy such republics, the world into 500 (*System*, IV, 270–71). Comte carefully computed such things as the ratio of patricians to proletarians and the proportion of agriculture to industry within each unit. He also gave detailed plans for regulating everything from industry to population. For example, he not only prescribed population control by delayed or chaste marriages, but also wanted to regulate "the quality of man's offspring" (*System*, IV, 278)—an ominous foreshadowing of the Nazi interest in creating the super-race.

In this Positivist sociocracy science and industry would develop hand in hand—both, of course, controlled by the moral injunctions of the Religion of Humanity. Under the Positivist regime, intellectual activity would be channeled, and technical research expedited. In the hands of the most capable engineers, industry would be developed efficiently and production regulated to avoid such "pathological states" as crises of overproduction. The great hostility between laborers and capitalists would of necessity disappear as, under the Positivist influence, each of these goups would come to a fuller sense of its social obligations.

In the Positivist sociocracy, the temporal order would resolve itself into two classes, Patriciate and Proletariat. (As we have seen in the table on p. 108, the middle classes would be absorbed into the group above or below them.) While these two classes would continue to perform their basic functions of management and labor, Comte projected fundamental changes in their attitudes, in their relationship, and, particularly for the poor, in the conditions of life.

Just as the concentration of political power seemed to Comte both natural and desirable, the concentration of capital in the hands of a few seemed to him the due reward of organizational ability and the guarantee of industrial efficiency. To remove the evils of capitalism while retaining its advantages, Comte therefore proposed to direct Positivist energies toward the cultivation of a sense of responsibility—the *noblesse oblige* of capitalism. Foremost among Positivist teachings, then, was the idea that wealth was a public trust: the rich had no right to be idle, no right to squander profits, no right to deal arrogantly with those less fortunate than they. On the contrary, the wealthy did have an obligation to use their power and possessions wisely—that is, to improve production and operation and to share profits with the workers. As an alternative to involvement in industry, those of the rich who were not employers might elect to be "knights" of the new Chivalry, an order dedicated to the relief of economic oppression. In effect, Comte regarded the capitalist as a public functionary—not legally, as he would be under communism or socialism, but morally. To cultivate this serious sense of social responsibility was the task of Positivist education; to enforce it was the task of organized public opinion.

Recognizing that inherited wealth does not always go to the most worthy or most capable, Comte proposed that the Sociocracy help the natural process and assist by private subscription or by State subsidy talented persons without money. The passing on of fortunes (like that of political power) would be up to the individual, but Comte stressed the responsibility that such a decision entailed. However much Comte wanted to strengthen the family, he encouraged an inheritance setup in which each individual would have to prove himself. A father owes his sons a good education and a start in life, Comte wrote, but a man should be free to leave his fortune to any persons he thinks may make the best use of it. In fact, adults would be encouraged to adopt children, not only to satisfy their need for a family, but to ensure a more adequate succession. Through all of these proposals Comte aimed at creating the inner motivation and supplying the external pressures which he felt could alone turn the selfish ambition of the enterprising into social channels.

The Proletariat, larger by far than the Patriciate, represented to Comte not only the potential spiritual power we have already discussed, but also the great productive force of the Sociocracy. Despite the urgent needs of the working people, the changes Comte wanted to bring about had (as in the case of the Patriciate) to begin with new mental attitudes. To instill a sense of pride in the poor, Comte stressed the dignity of work. In keeping with his idea that the Great Being encompassed the whole Chain of Being from the leaders to the humble animals that cooperate in society's progress, Comte emphasized that each individual of the Great Being had its own worth. Part of Comte's aim, then, was to give each individual a sense of his own dignity and a recognition of his part in this great project, the humanization of mankind. In addition to this, Positivism was to inculcate the idea that work (like capital) was a social obligation. As a contribution to society, work was to be seen as a good in itself. It was not to be something done for pay, but it would be performed gratuitously—as a social duty. Anti-Protestant though he was, Comte seems to have thoroughly approved of the "Protestant work ethic."

Along with these changes in self-image and in the attitude toward work, there would also be changes in the relationship of the workers to other classes. In the first place, the new educational system would offer mobility: out of the ranks of the workers would come many of the spiritual, political, and industrial leaders of the future. Comte envisioned an open caste system as providing the most favorable milieu for developing talent and rewarding merit. But, even more important than this, the dual order of the Sociocracy provided a measure of merit over and above political or economic success.

Nevertheless, the emphasis of Positivism was not altogether on spiritual values: the Sociocracy was also to provide strikingly different conditions of life for the worker. Comte's moral sense was offended by the idea of determining wages by competition in the marketplace, and he set himself to work out a fair system of recompense. For Comte, an equitable distribution of wealth had to consist of two parts: the "basics" for each family, and the "wages" arranged with the employer. While Comte always hesitated to talk about "rights," he did regard the worker as entitled to certain "basics"— that is, a decent home, subsistence, education, and medical care. The house (typically seven rooms for a family) was to be owned by the worker; the remaining benefits the State would provide. The "wages," which were to be negotiated with the employer, were to consist of two parts: a fixed monthly sum, and a sum proportionate to the worker's production (*System*, IV, 296–99). Thus, the laborer would be protected from the miseries of poverty—from hunger, cold, sickness, and degradation. The real duty of society to the poor, wrote Comte in a Shavian vein, is not in charity, but in creating conditions of life, education, and work conformable with human dignity (HM, 781).

This, then, was the Sociocracy in which mankind would fulfill its destiny. And this projection of a society fused into a harmonious, smoothly functioning organism was, for Comte, a scientific prevision rather than a mystical utopian dream. The thirty-three years have passed several times over and the promised land still has not been reached. Are we destined ever to attain this goal—to manage to create conditions of life, education, and work conformable with human dignity?

Over the years almost every major point Comte made has encountered both praise and criticism—and it is not difficult to see why *The System of Positive Polity* has been particularly vulnerable to the latter. Raymond Aron, in his book *Main Currents in Sociological Thought*,[9] discusses some of the reasons why Comte's conception of industrial society remained "outside the mainstream of modern social thought" even though his concerns are closer to today's than are many other nineteenth-century doctrines. Aron remarks that while "the leading ideas [of Comte's theory] are profound, his detailed description of industrial society is often liable to ridicule. . . . Moreover, Comte's conception of industrial society is linked to the belief that war is an anachronism." (What can we say of a philosophy of history that predicted in 1840 the disappearance of war from Western Europe?) Is it simply that the forces of egotism, empiricism, and anarchy are more resistant than Comte supposed? Or is it, Aron asks, that the twentieth century is not convinced of the merits Comte saw in the industrial society? Or is it that the world is not quite ready for habits of goodness for its own sake? Above all, Comte had, Aron points out, "laid the greatest emphasis on the reform of the temporal organization by the spiritual power.

The latter was to be the concern of scientists and philosophers, who were to replace the priests. . . . Now, it is probably on this point that history has disappointed Comte's disciples most harshly. Even if the temporal organization of industrial society is similar to what Comte imagined, the spiritual power of the philosopher and scientist is not yet born."[10]

Despite Comte's insights into the nature and problems of modern society, then, he seriously underestimated the strength of conflicting ideologies and of ingrained habits of behavior (war and conquest, for example). And, unfortunately, today's industrial societies seem little closer than those of the nineteenth century to solving the problems Comte delineated. If anything, the needs and the urgency seem even greater now than they were then. There is a familiar ring to Comte's complaints about the lack of moral and intellectual leadership, the fluctuations of power, the spread of corruption, and the concentration of government on the maintenance of "material order." "In this provisional state of affairs," Comte wrote,

when the official system declines the spiritual reorganization for which it feels its own unfitness, the intellectual and moral authority falls into the hands of anybody who will accept it, without any security of personal aptitude in regard to the most important and difficult problems that have ever engaged or can engage human thought: hence the reign of journalism, in the hands of literary men and lawyers, and the hopeless anarchy which some of them propose and all of them, in their collective capacity, illustrate. (HM, 748–49)

The activities of these self-proclaimed leaders constitute a kind of imperfect recognition, added Comte, of "the proper priority of intellectual and moral regeneration over mere political experiment, . . ." but do not add up to a real moral force. Comte foresaw only continuing anarchy and the extension of the social crisis so long as such conditions should prevail.

As for the Religion of Humanity, it proved from the beginning to be more effective in dividing than in unifying people. Early on, there were serious disagreements between "loyal Positivists" in both France and England regarding the particulars of the Comtean cult. These differences led to acrimonious fights and eventually both groups split into rival camps. In all, the record of Positivism in the nineteenth century affords scant evidence that the Religion of Humanity could create the kind of unity Comte had envisioned. W. M. Simon, in his survey of *European Positivism in the Nineteenth*

Century, points out the "palpable absurdities of Comte's lucubra-
tions" on such subjects as "fetishism, the utopia of the Virgin-
Mother, number mysticism, the nature of historical determinism,
the proposal for a 'Religious League' between Positivism and the
Roman Catholic Church."[11] Such odd ideas were bound to create
difficulties for disciples and provided easy targets for those who
wished to mock the Religion of Humanity. In view of the many
grounds of objection, it would seem something of a miracle that the
Positivist Church existed at all. By the early twentieth century, the
general view was that Comte had been significant for his Positive
philosophy—that is, for his philosophy of history, his classification
of the sciences, and his founding of sociology—but not for his Religion of Humanity.

But recent studies of Comte have gone back to the Religion of
Humanity to examine the religion itself and its import. Two examples will suffice to show the reevaluation of Comte's work: neither
of these studies is partisan, yet each suggests in its own way why
the religious aspect of Positivism deserves serious attention.

The first example comes from Raymond Aron's *Main Currents in
Sociological Thought*. Though the book focuses on sociological issues, Aron touches interestingly on Comtean religion. In its broad
outline the Religion of Humanity "is not so absurd," Aron says, "as
is generally believed. . . . If one insists on deriving a religion from
sociology (which I do not)," Aron continues,

the only one that seems to me thinkable, were I forced to do so, is that of
Auguste Comte, because it does not instruct us to love one society among
others, which would be tribal fanaticism, or to love the social order of the
future, which no one knows and in whose name one begins by exterminating
all skeptics. What Comte wanted us to love is neither the French society
of today, nor the Russian society of tomorrow, nor the American society
of the day after tomorrow, but the essential humanity which certain men
have been able to achieve and toward which all men should raise themselves. Perhaps this is not a "love object" which readily affects most men;
but of all the sociological religions, Comte's sociocracy seems to me phil-
osophically the best.[12]

Thus Aron, in focusing on the broad outline of Positivist religion,
draws attention to its nobler aspects.

A far darker view of the Religion of Humanity is taken by Eric
Voegelin in his book *From Enlightenment to Revolution*. His sober
evaluation of Comte begins with the claim that Comte's most original

contribution lies not in the Positive philosophy, but that "the real
significance of Comte in the history of the Western crisis . . . [is]
in his creativeness as a religious personality."[13] While Voegelin
points out the limitations and dangers of Comte's intramundane
religion (and of others like it), he shows the perceptiveness of
Comte's insight into the crisis of his—and our—time. Unlike the
"intellectual Positivists," Comte understood that the crisis was not
political, nor yet intellectual, but profoundly spiritual. Comte's
megalomania led him to suppose that he could regenerate society—
that through him France, at least, was about to enter the definitive,
i.e., the Positivist, state. Through himself, Comte believed, the
whole process of intuiting, elaborating, and concretizing man's spiritual destiny had been realized. Comte's obsessive need to reveal
all of his experiences and to record every nuance of his thought is
related to the fact that in his mind "the personal 'renovation' . . .
merges with social 'regeneration' into the one process of progressing
mankind. The life of the *Grand Être*, of Divine Humanity, streams
through the life of Comte. Every phase of this life is a divine manifestation since in this life is revealed the new, positivist phase of
the *Grand Être*. This revelation is not a personal event but the
public, historical coming of the new age, overflowing from the focal
point of the revelation into ever-widening circles of humanity. The
life of Comte is a true apocalypse in the religious sense of the
word."[14]

Through works such as these two studies we begin to understand
Positivism and its implications more fully. And, as a corollary, we
begin to see why intelligent contemporaries of Comte were drawn
to, or irritated by, the Religion of Humanity. On the one hand,
Aron points out the aspect which might appeal to people on a rational
or pragmatic level. Voegelin, on the other hand, is interested in
Comte's awareness of and response to deep-lying spiritual needs.
Aron concludes, somewhat wryly, that perhaps the reason the Religion of Humanity failed to carry the day is that it "is difficult for
men to love what would unite them and not to love what divides
them, once they no longer love transcendent realities."[15] For his
part, Voegelin concludes, even more soberingly, that if men no
longer have transcendent realities to love, they will invent them—
or a reasonable facsimile, the superman. From this viewpoint the
implications of Comte's life and work reach far beyond his actual
impact to touch us here and now. Through Comte, we are made
conscious of the nightmare coiled up inside the enlightenment

dream—the nightmare of reason derailed, of energies perverted, and of the spirit diseased. "In the present state of the crisis," writes Voegelin,

> we cannot know whether Comte is a forerunner of the apocalyptic founders of new realms whom we have witnessed in our time and of more formidable ones who will appear in the future, or whether the contemporary apocalyptic figures are the last ones of a breed of which Comte is by intellect and personal style the most grandiose specimen. Whatever the answer of the future will be, there can be no doubt even now that Comte belongs, with Marx, Lenin, and Hitler, to the series of men who would save mankind and themselves by divinizing their particular existence and imposing its law as the new order of society. The satanic Apocalypse of Man begins with Comte and has become the signature of the Western crisis.[16]

Comte's religion and polity can thus be seen as appealing either to mankind's nobler instincts or to its weaker side—or perhaps, as Comte might well point out, to both, since human nature is no less contradictory. What is most disturbing to us is that in the end Comte's system is geared primarily to the weakness—the natural irresoluteness which makes the injunctions of authority and submission to it necessary to individual happiness and social well-being (*System*, IV, 69). We can trace out here the same pattern, the same shift of emphasis, that we discerned in the Positive philosophy.

What Comte had undertaken as a youth (in 1822) was to search out the objective principles governing the external world and the human world (individual and social). Science and its methodology would, he was sure, ultimately give up those secrets: it would reveal its unity, and such knowledge would enable man to control life more effectively. Comte came to the conclusion, however, that there was only one way to achieve (comprehensive) unity: unity depended on the "subjective method." At the same time, as his search for unity became more obsessive, Comte stressed more and more that what science teaches us is, *above all*, "wise submission" to nature's laws.

The shift in emphasis had important political and moral implications as well. What began as a search for freedom and progress finally locates these goals in "willing submission" to discipline and to the order established by the spiritual and temporal authorities. What began with an insistence on the spiritual nature of man and with a quasi-Romantic view of mankind's innate altruism ended with individual and social well-being depending upon submission to a single spiritual authority. "All spiritual authority," Comte wrote, "necessarily originates in a single brain, and radiates thence gradually in every direction whatsoever . . ." (*System*, IV, 70). Here is the subjective synthesis, with a vengeance.

Thus Comte, with Napoleonic assurance, arrogated to himself spiritual power. Because Comte identified his politics and religion with scientific knowledge and its methodology, Positivism almost came to mean scientism. But, as Voegelin points out, Comte's polity, like his philosophy, can best be understood as a vision, and as a meditation on that vision. Since Comte's "apocalyptic vision" is not likely to be the last of the line, it is important to understand the assumptions and to be aware of the end to which the Positive religion and polity—and other such visions—lead. For men of compelling vision, like Blake's angel, impose their metaphysics on the unsuspecting.

CHAPTER 5

Positive Aesthetics

THOSE familiar only with the Comte of the *Positive Philosophy* would, no doubt, find the idea of a Positivist aesthetics astonishing. He himself commented on his neglect of this subject in his early works and began to remedy that lack by devoting a chapter of the *General View* to "the relation of art to Positivism." With his customary zeal for order and completeness, Comte there made art an integral part of his system and attributed to it a leading role in the institution of the new Positivist society. But the development of his aesthetic ideas was not yet complete: in the *Subjective Synthesis* the work of the philosopher and that of the artist merge so that in Comte's final vision one became almost indistinguishable from the other.

These discernible changes in Comte's attitude toward art are related to the shift from objective to subjective method in his philosophic system. And, as we found with the Positivist philosophy, the shift of emphasis left his theories open to a broad range of interpretations. Difficult as it is, however, to pin down Comte to a unified aesthetic theory, the sorting out of his main ideas regarding the principles and functions of art helps us understand the steps leading to his final philosophy. Such an examination sheds light as well on significant issues for nineteenth-century artists.

I *Comte's Evolving Aesthetic Theory*

Comte's early works focused on the intellect, and his explication of the law of the three stages and the classification of the sciences took little note of art. His insistence, in the Positive philosophy, that imagination must always be subordinate to observation seemed, indeed, to register an antipathy to the free play of imagination (HM, 803). Then, too, Comte's emphasis on scientific (intellectual) de-

velopment as the main index of progress seemed to discount the
possibility—that civilizations might be adjudged advanced on other
grounds—because of their moral or aesthetic development, for example. The evaluations implied by Comte's methodology and by his
standard of judgment are corroborated by his frequently expressed
scorn for the "mere literary men" and vain academicians produced
by the contemporary artistic establishment.[1] Taken all together,
Comte's general reticence on the subject of art and his negative
comments conveyed the impression that Positivism and art were
incompatible.

In the sketch of sociology which concludes the *Positive Philosophy*, however, we can discern signs of an awakening interest in art.
As Comte dealt with the progress of civilization, he had to take into
account artistic development and to consider its part in that pattern
of progress. Later, when he dealt more thoroughly with art's role
in the various historical stages (*System*, vols. I–III), Comte was to
discuss aesthetic development with reference to three basic functions: imitation, idealization, and expression. But in this preliminary
survey, it was, interestingly enough, the third of these functions
which he seized upon.

Comte began with the theory that fetishism, endowing the whole
universe with life, naturally favored the expansion of human imagination. And, as a corollary, he observed that "the fact to be shown
is that, in social as in individual life, the rise and expansion of human
faculties begins with the faculties of expression, so as gradually to
lead on the evolution of the superior . . . faculties . . ." (HM,
552). Thus early man, striving to express feelings and ideas, did so
first through gesture and image (i.e., "art"), and then through language.[2]

In this view, art is seen as the mediator between two important
aspects of the personality—Feelings and Intellect. And, by providing the means of expression, art touches the third fundamental
aspect of human nature by motivating Action. Though his treatment
here is brief, Comte's statement really grants to art two important
functions: it helps to integrate personality; and, in making possible
communication through image and sign, art thereby makes possible
civilization itself.

It was again the expressive nature of art that caught Comte's eye
when he came to his discussion of the Middle Ages. He singled out
the cathedrals as "the most perfect monumental expression of the
ideas and feelings of our moral nature" (HM, 632). These edifices,

splendid in themselves, also served to bring together the other arts—all the musical and artistic treasures of the time. Through these masterpieces, the cathedrals "expressed" the high spiritual aspirations of mankind. This expression, in turn, enabled the Medieval Church (despite its untenable doctrines) to extend its influence beyond the bounds of a particular community, or nation, or time. In this description, Comte draws attention again to the double meaning of expression. In this case, art's first function is to integrate the community (as it does the personality) by reflecting its feelings and ideas and by motivating its common actions. Even as it fulfills this function, art also serves as the instrument of the propagation of these feelings and ideas.

However striking the development of art was in those early periods, its progress was hampered, Comte held, because of the limitations imposed by the cultural context. Just as the living body is, to a great extent, "determined" by its milieu, art develops out of and relates to its particular time and place. Under fetishism, it was the lack of a cohesive society that hindered artistic development. The large-scale accomplishments of the Medieval Church, for example, would be impossible. As for the Medieval Church, its artistic possibilities were limited by the intellectual weakness of its dogmas. Though the artistic works of early civilization might seem barbaric to later critics, those achievements could only be appreciated in their relationship to the total culture; and when taken in context, such works might well attain "perfection."[3]

It was, in fact, the cultural context that Comte blamed for the failure of "modern" art. The inferiority of modern art, wrote this apostle of progress, cannot be attributed to "the decay of the aesthetic faculties in Man," but results from the "instability of Man's social condition." "Art could not grow up and expand on elements which were dissolving day by day" (HM, 709, 711). That is to say, modern artists merely bore the marks of the diseases of their time— confusion, vanity, materialism, and purposelessness. For art to flourish, said Comte, certain social conditions are requisite: "Not only must the social state be very marked, but it must also be permanent, to favor the effect of the fine arts; because that effect requires a close and established harmony between the interpreter and the spectator" (HM, 709). Comte's assumptions here are noteworthy: for him art is a social act, and one which can only be effective when the relationships between artist, spectator, and society are harmonious and stable.

In the *Positive Philosophy*, Comte did not develop these ideas about art to any great extent. The most that can be said for his brief acknowledgment of art there is that it affirms the importance of art and emphasizes its relative nature. All in all, Comte showed little evidence of artistic sensibility in his early works: he neither allotted much space (or attention) to it, nor did he show much sensitivity to style in his own involuted, iterative prose.[4]

As Comte began work on his systematization of the Positive polity, he took up the subject of art with the intent to remedy these defects and to show that "the new doctrine by the very fact of embracing the whole range of human relations in the spirit of reality, discloses the true theory of Art, which has hitherto been so great a deficiency in our speculative conceptions" (*System*, I, 4).

Comte's new approach can first be seen in his chapter on the relation of Positivism to art. In this section Comte proposed to spell out his definition of art, lay out its systematic principles, examine its functions, and project the role of art in bringing about the Positivist state of the future. In the remaining volumes of the *System*, Comte also expanded his treatment of art. At this point, art took an important place in his history and in his pattern for the Positivist state of the future. Another substantial section of the *System* elaborated Comte's views regarding the development of language and its relationship to art (*System*, II, ch. IV). And finally, the Positivist Library—Comte's list of great books—demonstrates a number of Comte's theories in action. Altogether, the subject of art is intricately woven into the unlikely fabric of the *System of Positive Polity*.

This new attention to art reflects the already noted shift from objective to subjective method in Comte's philosophy. The dominant role proposed for feelings in Positivist religion and society naturally led Comte to reflect on art, which had its origins in and directed itself to the emotional part of human nature. But where the *Positive Philosophy* had focused on the expressive nature of art, the key word in the *System of Positive Polity* seems to be *idealization*. Once Comte has so defined art, its functions and its role (present and future) become clear.

Comte's starting point was, then, his definition of art as an "ideal representation of Fact; its purpose being to cultivate our sense of perfection" (*System*, I, 227). This definition begins with art as a "representation of Fact" (i.e., imitation), but stresses idealization as the most important of art's "three distinct degrees or phases"—imitation, idealization, and expression.

"Art begins at first with simple Imitation," for the real is always "the source of the ideal" (*System*, I, 231). Next, the artist idealizes—that is, he makes the representation more beautiful and "in reality more faithful, because the principal features are brought prominently forward, instead of being obscured by a mass of unmeaning detail" (*System*, I, 231–32). And finally, there is Expression, "without which, the product of the imagination could not be communicated to others" (*System*, I, 232). Of these three stages, the second, idealization, represented to Comte (at least at this point) the "creative process which is the chief characteristic of Art" (*System*, I, 232). Idealization seemed to him superior to simple mirroring; while Expression, the concrete representation of the artist's mental picture or concept, seemed to be associated, in this discussion, with "labor" and technical skill.

Indeed, the idea that art is idealization is a central theme throughout Comte's chapter on the relation of Positivism to art. "Art always imitates, and always idealizes," he tells us (*System*, I, 231). And he tells us so again: Art's "special function is to idealize and stimulate"; expression acts on the feelings and "the effect is far greater when the representation . . . is suitably idealized" (*System*, I, 224, 228). Comte carefully tells us, too, that this idealization is not just the cultivation of beauty for its own sake; it is instead the quality which makes art the intermediary between intellect and action.

Both science (or philosophy as Comte used the term) and art begin with observation of the real world, the world of fact. Science seeks to explain that world, art to beautify it. But scientific concepts resemble artistic ones in important ways. Both begin with the imagining of a type or construct. Both, in conformity with the subjective principle, seek to ameliorate the world—though they operate in different ways to bring about that end. Science (or philosophy) represents the work of the intellect: observation, analysis, and the discovery of the natural laws governing phenomena. The facts and laws of science provide a coherent dogma which is the basis of intellectual conviction and therefore the source of intellectual unity. On the other hand, art, while it depends on the observations and insights of philosophy, also originates in and reaches out to touch the feelings, the only motivators of action. Art's function, then, as Comte conceived it, was to mediate between intellect and action

and hence to form the link between the Positivist philosophy and
the polity.

In general terms, the province of poetry, at once personal and
social, was to "modify our moral nature" (*System*, I, 230), to "charm
and elevate human life" (*System*, I, 225), to construct types of the
noblest kind, to elevate our feelings, and to "surpass realities so as
to stimulate us to amend them" (*System*, I, 228). And, much more
specifically, art's task was to regulate "the formation of social Utopias"—not the imaginary kind, of course, but "the natural order of
the future as revealed by the past" (*System*, I, 229). Because the
artist could create distinct, concrete images of the future, his prophetic pictures could stimulate the actions necessary to bring about
the regeneration of society (*System*, I, 228). In a word, the artist
was to help propagate Comte's new theories and to reinforce those
truths once the Positivist regime was established. Comte's early
views of art (as combining feelings, ideas, and actions; as related to
the cultural context; as a social action) thus merge in this new view
of art as the ideal instrument of propaganda.

Such ideas regarding art led Comte to give special emphasis to
it in the early years of the educational program he devised. Familiarity with the broad range of all arts—in all times and in all places—
would, he felt, cultivate the child's sense of Humanity as an integral
whole. Then, too, the habits of contemplation and meditation stimulated by art would also prepare the student for the exercise of these
disciplines in the next stage of education devoted to science. In the
"afterwork of education," art would join with religion to recall men
and women to those high feelings and principles it had first incul-
cated. To this end, the Religion of Humanity would rely on art's
forms and images in its worship ceremonies, but most of all in the
"spontaneous festivals," themselves large-scale works of art combining the four arts of poetry, music, painting, and sculpture (*System*, I, 243–44). Here Positivism would, no doubt, out-shine its
great forerunner, the Medieval Church. Ultimately, the unity of
civilization would find its fullest expression in a universal language
(*System*, II, 219–20).[5]

While these aspects of Positivism seem, on the whole, favorable
to art, two curious features suggest that Comte had certain reservations about it. The first point has to do with artists and their
training, the second with the Positivist Library.

Comte's hostility to the academies led him to propose that they be abolished. Artists, under the Positivist regime, would receive only the general aesthetic education. In the few cases where the particular art calls for a high degree of technical skill, the general education would be supplemented by some years of apprenticeship. Comte believed that under Positivism artists as a class would disappear and that as a result art would become more spontaneous and more closely integrated with the other aspects of life. He expected that within each of the groups comprising the spiritual leadership (the priesthood, the women, the workers) talented individuals would appear and give expression to the feelings and aspirations related to that group's role. Though Comte did not count on much celebration of energy from the workers, he did believe that women would cultivate the arts dedicated to sensibility and to domestic life. Naturally, the highest forms of public art (epic and drama, for example) would come from the priests (or from talented individuals who, though they lacked the dedication necessary to be priests, were, because of their gifts, more or less associate members of the priesthood). From all of this, it would seem that Comte had little sense of the difference between amateurism and professionalism in art; and it is clear, too, that he meant to encourage art only along certain specific lines.

The second point is a more general one. Comte's attention to education would lead us to suppose that his system would certainly encourage reading, and thus support literature. Yet we find, with a shock, not only that the habit of reading is to be discouraged, but also that Comte proposed "the systematic destruction of the accumulations which now compress or misdirect thought" (*System*, IV, 236–37). Never one to neglect his duty, Comte was quite willing to make the judgments necessary in such a proceeding. As a start, he drew up a list of 150 volumes which he felt deserved to survive. He suggested that the Positivist Library might well be reduced to 100 volumes, and that this number of books was sufficient even for a priest.

Although the proliferation of books may tempt us at times to regard this kind of selectivity as a clear boon, Comte's proposal for this great book-burning seems crudely inquisitional and altogether retrograde. The reasons given for this wholesale destruction again point up the totalitarian nature of Comte's system. In the first place, the encyclopedic education has no place for "idle questions," but it should be limited to only as much analysis as prepares for the

"synthetic construction" (*System*, IV, 236). That is, speculation is
to be limited in accordance with the exigencies of the subjective
synthesis. Whatever is not useful to this end should be ruthlessly
destroyed.

The regime described, so far from encouraging the habit of reading, makes
all feel to what extent it hampers meditation, the only real aid to which is
to be found in the inexhaustible study of the master-works of poetry, in-
variably in relation with the problem of man's existence.
   Guided by the hints I have given, the true Positivist may, even if a priest,
reduce his library to a hundred volumes. Philosophy is condensed into ten,
poetry into twenty more; another twenty will suffice for the whole of our
concrete conceptions, the data required for industrial purposes, natural
history, and the knowledge of the past. The second half of the collection
will be devoted to the monumental works which deserve from their original
merit to survive the systematic destruction of the accumulations which now
compress or misdirect thought. (*System*, IV, 236–37)

While Comte talked of the inexhaustible study of the master-works
of poetry, he meant specifically those culled out by the High Priest
as worthy. The chosen few in the Positivist Library, which seem at
first simply to represent an archetypal great-books list, turn out to
be the sole survivors of a holocaust. (In this connection, it should
be noted that Comte also arrogantly proposed the extermination of
all inferior life forms which did not contribute positively to Humanity's progress.) It is odd that Comte's study of history failed to
teach him that book-burning does not necessarily put an end to
dissenting ideas. At any rate, this proposal can hardly be called
encouraging to the art of literature.
   The Positivist Library, as Comte described it, was presumably
an adjunct of the educational system, and would provide highly
selected materials for learning and for meditation. In reality, however, the Library's primary function was to help maintain the
authority of the priesthood. In the first place, by discouraging independent reading, Comte's system accustomed the student to rely
on the information channeled through the priests, who might field
questions or declare them out of bounds at their own convenience.
In the second place, this "voluntary submission" to priestly authority
was to be further reinforced by the rigorous judgments implicit in
both the Positive Calendar and the Positive Library. "Calendar and
Library—by the aid of the two," Comte wrote, "the priesthood of
Humanity will lay the groundwork of its ascendancy over the living

by its judgment of the dead, during the first phase of the organic transition" (*System*, IV, 353). While the names remaining on these lists were to be venerated, they, like those in Dante's *Divine Comedy*, would serve as ever-present reminders of the dread process of last judgment. In Comte's universe, however, the last word was to be pronounced not by God, but by Positivism's High Priest.

In the overall picture, Comte's claim that Positivism would create conditions favorable to art has to be offset by the limits implicit in his view of art (as propaganda), in the educational program itself, and in the proposed destruction of books not fitting into the system. Positivism would, on the other hand, supply the comprehensive and coherent system of beliefs Comte (and many artists also) regarded as necessary to art's flourishing, and it would provide noble concepts for the artist to embellish. Beyond this, by making the artist an "accessory member" of the spiritual power, Positivism would give artists a meaningful "real vocation" (*System*, I, 224).

In the *Subjective Synthesis* Comte seems to have stepped out into the strange world of dream. The book begins with a mild fantasy— a prevision, Comte would have said—a projection into the world of the twentieth century when the Positivist state would presumably be well established. Although the subject of the book is mathematics as it should be taught by the priests in this future state, what is relevant to our purposes here is Comte's development of the subjective synthesis and its relationship to the creative imagination of the artist.[6]

In this first stage of the Positive philosophy revisited, Comte began reworking that philosophy—reordering the hierarchy of the sciences, revising the old methodology, and aiming at the final systematization.

The reordering of the hierarchy (already proposed in the *System of Positive Polity*) gave Comte a completed system of seven sciences: mathematics, astronomy, physics, chemistry, biology, sociology, and moral science. Having dealt with the last and most important of these, the moral science, in his *System*, Comte circled back to establish the framework, at least, of his completed philosophy by applying the subjective method to the basic science, mathematics.

At this point in Comte's thinking, the intellect, which in the early works had seemed to be the great faculty offering hope of progress, now appeared to him to represent the greatest obstacle to humanity's amelioration. And, the more Comte came to regard the intellect as

proud, anarchical, and dry, the more he sought to bend it to submission.[7] So it was that the subjective method, which at first meant
that all things should be evaluated in the light of human needs,
finally turned into the subjective synthesis and came to mean that
all things (including intellect) should be subordinated to feelings.
To this end Comte proposed a curious revival of fetishism to help
resolve the epistemological problems and to facilitate the creation
of a unified system.

Having failed in his search for unity through an objective synthesis, Comte looked elsewhere for a key to a unified system. Unwilling to accept either the alternative represented by materialism
(the reduction of all things to matter and mechanics), or that represented by idealism (the reduction of all things to mental phenomena), Comte opted instead to return to the primitive solution offered
by fetishism—a solution based on the idea that all things are animated by the same kind of life as human beings are (*Subjective
Synthesis*, 8).[8] Comte's version of fetishism did reserve intellect for
human beings: in the things of the external world, feelings and the
will to action operate blindly; in the human being, intellect is added.
Where Descartes had resorted to God as the necessary link between
mind and matter, Comte resorted to Humanity, whose collective
attainment is intellect, even while it shares the feelings and will of
matter.

The effect of Comte's return to fetishism was a neo-Romantic
emphasis on feeling (as shared by things and by humanity), on
spontaneity (the intuitive responses), and—in a surprising reversal
of the methodology of the *Positive Philosophy*—on imagination over
intellect. Though the dominance of intellect had been necessary in
order to bring science to the point where humanity might understand and modify the conditions of existence, it was now necessary,
Comte claimed, to discipline that unruly faculty. Despite mankind's
pride in intellectual accomplishments, these scientific efforts were,
and could only remain, fragmentary and dispersive. Just as egoism,
having first motivated mankind to improve the conditions of life, at
a later stage had to be subordinated to altruism; and just as progress,
having served its turn, had to be subordinated to order; intellect
must now be subordinated to feeling and to imagination in order
that the complete synthesis might be attained.

What is particularly new in Comte's thesis in the *Subjective Synthesis* is the role allotted to the imagination. The "new logic," which
is designed to escape the limitations of deduction and induction,

must be modeled, he said, on the "universal method" of poetic masterpieces, which subordinate these inferior methods to "construction" (*Subjective Synthesis*, 43–44).[9] The creative imagination is constructive in two senses, Comte continued: in its conception of a vast, coherent unity; and in the systematic, disciplined arrangement of its expression (*Subjective Synthesis*, 33, 47, 755).

Comte's new definition of Positivist logic particularly stressed the conception of ideas. He defined the new logic as "the normal bringing together (or coordination) of feelings, of images, and of signs in order to inspire in us the conceptions which relate to our needs, moral, intellectual, and physical (*Subjective Synthesis*, 27). Under the old logic, deduction and induction limited logic to the "discovery of truths that are expedient for us" (*Subjective Synthesis*, 27).[10] The new logic, Comte averred, would instead emphasize the subjective nature of intellectual constructs and the total extent of their domain—internal as well as external. The formula of the new logic is "induction for the sake of deduction, for the purpose of construction": *Induire pour déduire, afin de construire* (*Subjective Synthesis*, 44).

The epistemological problem that Comte was wrestling with had two aspects. The first difficulty arose from the imperfect nature of our empirical knowledge: since we have no knowledge of things-in-themselves (as Locke had pointed out, and as Berkeley and Hume insisted), we have no way of arriving at definitive knowledge about substances—or consequently about such things as causes. The second aspect is related to the first; our theoretical knowledge, too, is always imperfect in that it never really corresponds to the objective, empirical world. If all this be true, reasoned Comte, then we ought not only to recognize the subjective nature of all our intellectual constructs, but we ought to use this constructive power to further the cause of Humanity.

In coming back again to a discussion of hypothesis as a method, Comte this time put this method squarely in the field of fiction. He referred, for example, to his own hypotheses as "ces fictions" (*Subjective Synthesis*, 10, 11). (This statement does not, of course, prevent him from treating them as truths later on.) He wanted to remind us that a domain of fiction does exist and does have certain rules (*Subjective Synthesis*, 27).[11] Above all, he proposed "to systematize conjecture" as much as demonstration (*Subjective Synthesis*, 27).[12] With these premises in mind, then, Comte at one stroke freed hypothesis from its bondage: "disengaged from scientific empiricism," logic will no longer, he said, "restrict itself to the domain of verifiable hypotheses. . . ." Thus the "religious logic" of Positivism completes this science (logic) by extending it to the "domain, much more vast, and no less legitimate, of the conceptions calculated to develop feeling without shocking our reason" (*Subjective Synthesis*, 40).[13] In this new logic, a coherent, unified theory has its own kind of validity. But Comte's principal rule in developing hypotheses is simply that they be dedicated to society's well-being—the sole source of true unity.[14] Though hypotheses should not contradict known facts or laws, they need not be verifiable (i.e., subject to proof). This approach to science Mill found strange indeed.[15]

In accordance with these rules, Comte had developed his own "fundamental hypothesis"—that all things in the external world have the faculties of feeling and acting (though not of thinking). This neofetishism not only had the virtue of closing the mind-matter gap, but it provided Comte with a way of bridging another gap—that between science and moral action. In Comte's hypothesis, the Earth (the totality of external, objective things) becomes the *Grand-Fétiche;* the Earth has prepared itself for the Great Being of Humanity (the *Grand-Être*) and continues to assist Humanity in its amelioration of the universal order.[16] The "inalterable trinity" of Positivism is completed by Comte's concept of Space as the *Grand-Milieu*, the (subjective) "ether" or milieu in which all phenomena exist.[17] The concept of these three entities brings together the objective world and the subjective milieu through the intermediary of Humanity, at once objective and subjective. All three together provide the conditions of Humanity's progress. All three also operate together to teach mankind the lesson of submission—to objective laws (Earth); to society's collective good (Humanity); and to the immutable course of destiny (associated by Comte with Space) (*Subjective Synthesis*, 17–19, 35, 37, 53).[18]

In this fashion Comte pieced out the imperfections of our knowledge, theoretical and empirical, with his poetic fictions. For, he wrote, "it is necessary that the commandment assist the arrangement so that the order may be complete" (*Subjective Synthesis*, 25).[19] Under the aegis of social need/unity the philosopher-poet may create whatever fictions serve his purpose, provided only that these do not conflict with known facts or laws. Comte's own hypothesis about the Universe was based on the assumption that, given this concept of an all-embracing order and this sense of shared life, mankind might in fact be brought to realize—to understand and to complete—the final synthesis.

The final purpose of the philosopher is to communicate his conceptions forcefully and thereby stimulate feelings and activity. This end he accomplishes through the appropriate combination of signs (language) and images, and through the very structure of the work itself. Here again logic merges with poetry, just as philosophy and poetry flow together in the idealized vision and unified conception of the subjective synthesis. Comte now claimed that Positivism considered as a philosophy of science might produce intellectual conviction, but it could never work strongly enough on the feelings to motivate action. Such power belongs instead to poetry; therefore, art and, in the educational system, aesthetic appreciation provide the necessary links between intellect and heart.

For Comte, the images that poetry (or art) creates begin with idealizations of the real world—fictions designed to create the feelings that motivate action. But Comte's own fictions admittedly went beyond this idealization of the objective world: his concept of Space as the Grand Milieu, for example, was an attempt to give concreteness to what is subjective only. Comte proposed that we *picture* the Abstract Milieu as a green background on which we project our mental images, and that we attribute to it "all the objectivity of the most abstract laws" so that (the universal) order may be complete. The philosopher (and we) must utilize the concreteness and clarity of poetic images; for to poetry ultimately belongs "the task of making felt the efficacity of the institutions destined to generalize the human type and connect it to Matter [Earth] and to Space" (*Subjective Synthesis,* 25–26).[20] Here Comte was again deriving his model from Church practices: the traditional meditation begins with an exercise of memory and imagination in which the individual is to visualize or "compose" a place or event.[21] In the next step of meditation, the intellect guides the analysis of that which is imagined or remembered. Finally, the will moves the affections to respond positively. In Comte's version, it is the feelings that motivate action, nevertheless the pattern of meditation persists. As Louis Martz points out in his discussion of *The Meditative Poem,* "Meditation points toward poetry, in its use of images, in its technique of arousing the passionate affections of the will."[22] And, the image-making of the poet functions for society as memory and imagination do for the meditator. In this creative act, Comte added, the most powerful minds find their greatest power in adapting to their needs the "spontaneous logic" (feelings and images) of fetishism. Though Comte's own images are hardly compelling, we can understand his attempt to imitate such poets as Dante, for example, whose language and imagery sweep us along in their current whether we believe as he did, or not.

But the elaboration of concepts in art requires not only the use of appropriate images and signs, it involves the refinement of structure as well. The construction of a work, as Comte conceived of it, had to be governed (as poetry is) by the strict rule of number and had also to be related integrally to the meaning conveyed. The passages in which Comte discussed numbers reveal more starkly than anything else the obsessiveness of his concern with numbers, with unity, and with self-discipline.

Dante, to be sure, lured him along this path, but Comte succeeded in out-systematizing his master. At any rate, Comte did not rest content with adopting the number mysticism passed down from antiquity; he elaborated his own subjective theory of numbers and laid out a specific format ("plan") for "all important compositions."[23] This plan was not only set forth in the *Subjective Synthesis*, but it was exemplified in its structure as well.

Comte's subjective theory of numbers picked up the favorites of the mystics, for whom one, three, and seven, in particular, were often sacred numbers. One, being the number of synthesis, or unity, needed no further recommendation for Comte. Two was significant to him as the number of coordination. (Ultimately, Comte claimed, all combination is binary.) Three, the number of all progression was particularly sacred to him. Comte found the root of three's magic in the basic family: woman (love), man (order), and child (progress). (The subjective theory relates everything to the universal Positivist order.) Prime numbers all had an especial value in Comte's eyes because of their indivisibility—unity was always, in itself, meaningful to Comte. (For the same reason, double prime numbers— where the rank of a prime number is also a prime number—were even better.) The number seven, like three, had a particular magic for Comte. He explained its qualities: "Formed by two progressions followed by a synthesis, or of a progression between two pairs [or combinations], the number seven, coming after the sum of the three sacred numbers, determines the largest group we can distinctly imagine. Reciprocally, it marks the limit of the divisions which we can directly conceive in a magnitude of any kind" (*Subjective Synthesis*, 127).[24] Consequently, seven was to be the new basis for numeration under Positivism; to Comte, the difficulties of a septimal numbering system were irrelevant. This small sampling of Comte's number theory suffices to show the nature of his preoccupation with number. These examples also betray his predilection for system— to which he would, in the long run, sacrifice all.

But number theory was not just one of the subjects of the *Subjective Synthesis*, it provided the principles of structure for the book itself and for "all important compositions." Prime numbers, as we might expect, inspired Comte's plan—and the greatest of these was seven: each volume should have seven chapters (in addition to the introduction and conclusion); each chapter should have three parts; each of these three parts should have seven sections, each composed of seven groups of sentences. Comte even went so far as to prescribe the structure for these groups of sentences and for the individual sentences as well: "Normally constructed, the section offers a central group of seven sentences, which precede and follow three groups of five: the initial section of each part reduces to three sentences three of its symmetrically placed groups: the final section gives seven sentences to each of its extreme groups" (*Subjective Synthesis*, 755).[25] This rule of composition, Comte explained, "brings prose close to the regularity of poetry," especially if the writer obeys Comte's previous injunction to limit each sentence to five printed lines (i.e., 250 letters).

In contrast with these rules for important philosophic works were Comte's prescriptions for great poems. These ambitious poems would normally consist of thirteen—another magic number—cantos, broken down into parts, sections, and groups like Comte's chapters. While this poetic structure seems different from that prescribed for philosophic works, the two actually come to much the same plan: when the six cantos allotted to introduction and conclusion (three cantos each) are subtracted, the body of the poem consists of seven cantos, corresponding to the seven-part main section of the philosophic work. Comte also proposed a new plan for versification based on a seven-line stanza (*Subjective Synthesis*, 760).

If all this were not enough to discipline the pen, Comte superimposed on this arithmetical formula what he called an "algebraic" one. This added system of coordination was to depend on the writer's fashioning a kind of acrostic: each section was to be represented by a word of seven letters derived from the initial letter (of the first word of the first sentence) of each of its component groups. These acrostic words were to be carefully chosen to "offer a synthesizing or sympathetic meaning," and should "relate as much as possible, to the corresponding section or part." Comte further specified that, in reading, these words were to be pronounced so that "the phonic impression completes the graphic effect, following the example offered spontaneously by the poets to the philosophers" (*Subjective Synthesis*, 757).[26]

This veritable maze of arithmetic and algebraic formulae suggests that Comte regarded the philosopher as well as the artist as a fabulous artificer. Art seems to take on the aspect of a complex but mechanical game—delightful mainly because of its intricacy. Undoubtedly, the weaving of such artful constructions did appeal strongly to Comte because he saw in them a way of creating a vast web out of seemingly heterogeneous parts. But still more, art provided the supreme example of self-imposed discipline: the recurring theme in this volume is the lesson of voluntary submission. As the study of the objective world was, ultimately, to accustom us to the idea of graceful submission to (objective) natural law, so these rules of composition would teach us "how much the perfecting of the intelligence, like that of the feelings and of action, depends upon our worthy submission" (*Subjective Synthesis*, xiv).[27] In addition, the very difficulty of such work would, Comte felt, somehow guarantee the worthiness and dedication of the artist, and present a barrier to inferior souls. "It is necessary to social harmony," Comte wrote, "that the best forms of composition, philosophic or poetic, forbid it to the mediocre and even render it exceptional among the elite . . ." (*Subjective Synthesis*, 761).[28] The maze is, then, a trial and a test.

Thus, for Comte, not only does the history of art follow its own pattern of three stages, but, in society's "definitive" state, the great works he envisioned might be seen as an emblem for Positivism itself. Both try to coordinate all the human capacities. The spontaneous impulses and feelings which sought expression in gesture and then language are, no less, the sources of vitality and social life for "modern" man. From the welter of feelings, images, impressions, thoughts, and impulses, the artist seeks to draw a pattern—to create a synthesis. One model for this synthesis is found in the meditation tradition—in the systematizing of image-making so as to concentrate and coordinate the powers of imagination, understanding, and will. These exercises in contemplation put the individual in touch with the spiritual realm (the "divine" in the original tradition) and "stir us up to the love and exercise of virtue."[29] The other model is the maze, which, like the meditation, patterns the search for the elusive center—unity. The great works of art under Positivism would express the ultimate synthesis—reconciling the oppositions between feeling and intellect, subject and object, emotion and order, selfishness and altruism, individual and state. While achieving this end, artists would also stir the emotions which alone could motivate people to move toward this great unity; and, at the same time, they would demonstrate the attitude of "worthy submission" to rule— the kind of submission necessary to all if order and unity were to be achieved. Only the actions themselves which convert the dream into reality lie outside the work of art.

II *Positivism and Literature*

Given these progressive elaborations of Comte's thinking about art, we can hardly expect to find a simple, direct "influence" on the writers of his time.[30] At best, the problem of influence is a tricky one, and with Comte the difficulties are multiplied. In some cases it is impossible to tell whether Comte was simply reflecting attitudes of his time, or whether his was a decisive voice for a particular person or movement. Furthermore, as we have already indicated, the vast storehouse of Comtean ideas allowed individuals to choose those they found most pleasing. Nevertheless, there are certain Comtean ideas which seem to have had an impact on literature even though the writers concerned cannot really be called Positivists or disciples of Comte. Our discussion will focus on three major ways in which Comte's theories relate to or are adapted in literature and literary theory.

The nineteenth-century artistic movement Comte's name is most frequently associated with is Naturalism. The line of influence is traced back from Emile Zola, the propounder of the literary theory of Naturalism,[31] to Claude Bernard,[32] a doctor whose methodology in chemistry was carried over into literature by Zola. It is known that Bernard was familiar with Comte's *Positive Philosophy,* and it is clear that he, like Comte, was interested in scientific methodology. Whether Comte was a decisive influence on Bernard is, however, a moot question.[33] Certainly many of the scientists of this period were trying to refine terminology and establish reliable scientific methods. In this case it is possible that influence has been ascribed to Comte mainly because Positivism was a clearly defined movement representing the scientism of the time.

Certainly there are general likenesses between ideas in the *Positive Philosophy* and the literary theory of Naturalism. Both focus on the scientific methods of observation and experiment, and both stress the need for objectivity. Both deal with the relationship between the individual and the milieu; and, furthermore, both regard the future as predictable (though perhaps modifiable), given the orderly progression of past and present.[34]

Zola, in his discussion of "the Experimental Novel," quoted from Bernard to show how the process of observation and experiment works for the scientist, and then he added:

Now . . . we can see equally well that the novelist is both observer and experimenter. The observer in him presents data as he has observed them, determines the point of departure, establishes the solid ground on which his characters will stand and his phenomena take place. Then the experimenter appears and institutes the experiment, that is, sets the characters of a particular story in motion, in order to show that the series of events therein will be those demanded by the determinism of the phenomena under study. It is almost always an experiment "in order to see," as Claude Bernard puts it.

. . . In short, the whole operation consists of taking facts from nature, then studying the mechanism of the data by acting on them through a modification of circumstances and environment without ever departing from the laws of nature. At the end there is knowledge, scientific knowledge, of man in his individual and social action.[35]

Hence the novelist's method is an adaptation of the scientific method recommended by Comte as the way to experiment with living organisms (i.e., by modifying the milieu in which they live).

Zola also makes use of the "historical method." For him, this meant turning his microscope on successive generations of the Rougon-Macquart family, for example—a family whose genes and whose circumstances seemed to carry an inevitable destiny. To record these characters and their fates faithfully and objectively was Zola's aim. The sole task of the author, he claimed, is "to put true documents before your eyes" and to do so without "impassioned or tender intervention."[36] For Zola, the moral function of art was no different from that of science; both teach us "the lofty lesson of the real."[37]

Such an approach to art does seem to be in harmony with basic ideas found in the *Positive Philosophy*, where attention is focused on the external world—on the inevitability of its laws, and on the objective method of dealing with it. As we have noted, however, Comte's specific statements about art in this work did not follow precisely these lines. His tendency to stress expression and idealization over exact representation would hardly have satisfied the strict tenets of Naturalism as spelled out by Zola. Nevertheless, Comte did indicate that the artist's clear picture of present reality and its imperfections could influence people to try to change the world for the better.[38] And, after all, Comte and Zola were of one mind on an essential point—the central importance of "the lofty lesson of the real."

The second kind of Positivist influence on literature was more direct. Comte's discussion of idealization in *A General View of Positivism* related this function of art to prevision (i.e., scientific prediction of the future). By this means, Comte hoped to tie utopian literature closer to real life and to make it a useful instrument of propaganda. The utopian works of the late nineteenth and early twentieth centuries can hardly all be laid at Comte's door—Socialists and Communists could also easily perceive the advantage of this mode of propaganda. But, at any rate, the writer's gift of presenting "real life" vividly and of projecting future directions concretely attracted the attention of social planners, and artists themselves found in this new role of leadership a heady new sense of purpose.

The transmutation of ideas into fictional characters and events tends in itself to complicate and modify those ideas; nevertheless, we can often discern specific motifs and images which tie the fictions to their sources even when they are intermingled with other elements. Thus we find, for example, numerous Comtean motifs in the works of Edward Bellamy[39] and Bernard Shaw[40]—though both of them finally opted for forms of socialism rather than for the Positivist Republic of the West.

Bellamy, troubled by religious doubts in his youth, had developed his own Religion of Solidarity—a faith in altruism somewhat resembling that of the Religion of Humanity.[41] As Bellamy matured, his moral and religious ideas channeled into social and economic concerns. The literary result was the utopian vision of *Looking Backward* (1888) and *Equality* (1897); the practical result was his development of Nationalism, a political movement meant to begin the reorganization of society envisioned in his books.

Like Comte, Bellamy peered into the future to examine the new
state, which he thought was about to be born. In Bellamy's novel,
Julian West, through the power of mesmerism, travels to the wonderful twentieth century and back. The voyager sees a new world,
one which has evolved peaceably from the old through the force of
public opinion. That future society bears few of the disease marks
of the nineteenth century—none of its poverty, squalor, and strife.
Instead, progress, in its inevitable course, has brought about an
industrial and economic reorganization which, by shifting the economic base from competition to cooperation, has radically changed
all of life. In Bellamy's Utopia, industry is nationalized; all who are
able must work; all, able or not, share alike in the profits of industry.
The injustices and the dehumanization of the wage market are thus
avoided, and the dignity and well-being of each individual are assured. In Bellamy's fictions, then, we do not find the exact image
of Comte's sociocracy: neither Comte's version of capitalism, for
example, nor his specific apportionment of wages, nor his precise
ordering of hierarchies is reflected in *Looking Backward*. Nevertheless, Bellamy shared with Comte the view that the reform of
society was the one object worthy of man's efforts, that this change
could be effected by moral means (through public opinion), and that
this meliorism was dependent on the cultivation of the altruistic
instincts in human nature.[42] In both projections, the paternalistic
state would see to it that each citizen would be provided with education, health care, and subsistence (including "social security").
And, for both, this millennium-on-earth was but the beginning of
what Bellamy called a "whole infinity" of human development (physical, mental, and moral) stretching beyond it.[43]

As Sylvia Bowman points out in her study of *Edward Bellamy
Abroad*, this American writer reflected in his books "Comte's desire
to unite order with progress; to unify the past and the present into
a harmonious whole; to direct all the social forces to one end—moral
progress; and to subordinate all things to and establish all man-
willed evolutionary progress upon the basic universal principle of
love."[44] Bellamy was, perhaps, more optimistic regarding human
nature than Comte had been, for he dispensed with the religious
institutions Comte had so carefully designed to cultivate and reinforce altruism. But for Bellamy, as for Comte, the living representative of this nobler part of human nature was womankind: in
woman he saw the kind of "centripetal force which developed the

impersonal—unselfishness—in man which made solidarity and, therefore, true progress possible."[45]

The popularity of Bellamy's work and the discussion it engendered attest to the power of fiction to do exactly what Comte had said it was art's proper function to do—to affect feelings and ideas so as to bring about a new society. Bellamy's *Equality* vividly portrayed the devastating realities of capitalistic industrialism;[46] his *Looking Backward* made concrete a more human alternative. Together, these works showed the need for and the desirability of a new order. Through his imaginative fictions, Bellamy's ideas not only permeated American thought at the popular level, but they also influenced profoundly seminal figures in numerous fields—for example, John Dewey, in philosophy and in education; William Allen White, in journalism; Eugene V. Debs, in the labor movement; and Thorstein Veblen, in economics.[47] Abroad, too, Bellamy's influence was widespread.[48] John Dewey may not have been far wrong when he called Bellamy the Great American Prophet.

Another such prophet and polemicist was Bernard Shaw. Officially a Fabian Socialist,[49] Shaw had derived key ideas from both Comte and Bellamy (among others). Like them, Shaw devoted his energies to bringing about the next stage in society's progress through a new "spiritual" power. The displacement of the old order by the new is dramatized by Shaw in a variety of plays, ranging from *Major Barbara* to the myth-creating fantasia, *Back to Methuselah*.[50] The clearest example of Positivist influence is found in *Major Barbara*, a "contemporary-issue" play which deals with the problem of morality in an industrial society. Industry is represented in this play by the successful capitalist, Andrew Undershaft, plainly one of Comte's patriciate. Undershaft's daughter, Barbara, has, however, aligned herself with what seems to be the most vital "spiritual power" in modern society—the Salvation Army. The central conflict in the play is between the "enlightened capitalism" of Undershaft and the inadequate spiritual power of the Salvation Army, which, however pure in itself, can only alleviate the misery of the poor by receiving handouts from those industries responsible for the destitution in the first place. Undershaft first undercuts Barbara's idealistic beliefs by showing her that the real power behind the Salvation Army is, after all, industry and its money—moral or not. He then wins her over by showing her his alternative, a prosperous and beautiful industrial community. Seeing it, Barbara perceives that, for all its concern with material things, an efficiently organized and responsibly run industrial complex performs a spiritual function when it provides living and working conditions conformable with human dignity. A number of Comtean motifs are discernible in this play: the gradual emergence of a new order from the instabilities of the old; the interplay among intellect (Cusins), action (Undershaft), and social feeling (Barbara); and, in a playful turn, the choosing of a worthy heir by "adoption." But, even while using Comtean ideas, Shaw suggests that mankind must go beyond enlightened capitalism to a world not built on munitions-making, to a world whose goods are shared by all workers.[51]

While it is surely impossible to envision Shaw as a submissive disciple of the High Priest of Humanity, we can recognize, nonetheless, that Shaw shared many of Comte's assumptions—about the function of art in giving concreteness to ideas and in motivating action, about the role of the artist in bringing about humanity's progress, and about many of the particulars regarding the next stage of civilization.[52] Filtered through Shaw's sharply witty lines, these ideas seem but distantly related to those which emerge rather murkily from Comte's earnest prose. But the artist's task is, according to Comte, to concretize, to sharpen, and to give impact to concepts. The artist is "to construct types of the noblest kind"—to "surpass realities so as to stimulate us to amend them" (*System of Positive Polity*, I, 228). Shaw, whether writing plays or prefaces or pamphlets, certainly aimed to stimulate change and thereby to be a creative participant in the evolution of humanity. Like his own Major Barbara, and like Comte, he wanted to be part of a spiritual power effecting change in the real world.

The third kind of Positivist influence is more general and more complicated than the two we have already discussed. An appropriate representative of this group is George Eliot, whose relationship to Positivism has long been something of a puzzle. Her familiarity with Comte's work is easily documented;[53] yet W. M. Simon declares that, though he finds specifically Positivist ideas in Eliot's "College Breakfast Party" and in some of her poems, he could not "with the best will in the world . . . find more than a half-dozen brief passages each in *The Spanish Gypsy* and . . . *Daniel Deronda* which bear any sort of Positivist interpretation, and the principal message of both works is a paean to nationalism."[54] If, indeed, George Eliot committed herself to Positivism only in minor works, it would be true that Positivist influence on her writing has been greatly exaggerated.

Certainly George Eliot is not a propagandist in the vein of Shaw and Bellamy. And, we can only agree that Eliot's major works are not directly Positivist as her "College Breakfast Party" and "Let Me Join the Choir Invisible" are. Nevertheless, George Eliot's work is permeated with important Comtean ideas—ideas which she did not expound but tried to make "thoroughly incarnate" in the characters and situations of her novels. Furthermore, even when she declared herself unequal to the task of portraying in fiction the ideal Comtean society, she added, "On the other hand, my whole soul goes with your desire that it should be done, and I shall at least keep the great possibility (or impossibility) perpetually in my mind, as something towards which I must strive, though it may be that I can do so only in a fragmentary way."[55]

What we find in the novels of the 1860s and 1870s (the ones Simon particularly mentions) is this "fragmentary way" of embodying fundamental Comtean ideas. In these novels, Eliot's emphasis is always on moral and social issues: on the need actively to cultivate altruism over egoism; on the "lofty lesson of the real"; on the need for submission and discipline; on the concept of society as a living entity.

In *Middlemarch* and *Daniel Deronda,* the natural selfishness of individuals like Fred Vincy and Gwendolyn Harleth is brought up against the reality that each individual fate is inextricably intertwined with others. In both cases, the mentors (Mary Garth and Daniel Deronda) help to bring the egoists to recognize their moral stupidity, and thereby they help nurture the seeds of moral growth.[56]

Despite Eliot's belief that we are all born morally stupid, she was nonetheless convinced of "the relative goodness and nobleness of human dispositions and motives."[57] This double conviction provided the psychological basis for George Eliot's meliorism just as it did for Comte's. The need to actively cultivate this second aspect of human nature is what she said motivated her writing, as well: "And the inspiring principle which alone gives me courage to write is, that of so presenting our human life as to help my readers in getting a clearer conception and a more active admiration of those vital elements which bind men together and give a higher worthiness to their existence."[58]

This moral emphasis means that George Eliot was not committed to the objectivity of Naturalism. She did, however, try to portray the "exact truth" and placed herself in the "Dutch realism" class of art.[59] For Eliot, the first lesson of the real is the enlargement of human sympathy: "The only effect I ardently long to produce by my writings," she said, "is that those who read them should be better able to *imagine* and to *feel* the pains and joys of those who differ from themselves in everything but the broad fact of being struggling erring human creatures."[60]

Often the "lofty lesson" to be learned is that of submission or renunciation. In both *The Spanish Gypsy* and *Daniel Deronda,* what Simon reads as a "paean to nationalism" is, rather, the call to a duty beyond the self. The gypsy Fedalma's renunciation of love and marriage for "a great destiny," is, as George Eliot makes clear, a victory for altruism.[61] Her voluntary submission to duty opens up the possibility of moral and social evolution as the gypsy rule passes from the leadership of action (the father) to a leadership of greater sensibility (the daughter). Though Daniel Deronda does not give up love, he does renounce his comfortable upper-class existence to take his place with the despised Jews. But doing so enables him to become part of the great spiritual movement of Jewish Nationalism—a "type" or symbol of a more universal spiritual love (and state) to come.[62] In both stories, the main point is that the greater good lies in submission to duty.

In Eliot's novels, as in Comte, "submission to the real" or to duty is not passivity or paralysis: it simply means that plans must be based on reality, not illusion; it means that life can be shaped, though not created whole. As the narrator of *Middlemarch* points out, "It always remains true that if we had been greater, circumstance would have been less strong against us."[63]

Finally, Comte's all-encompassing unity—the oneness of world, society, and self—is reflected in George Eliot's work as well. In *Middlemarch,* for example, individuals and seemingly separate groups finally seem to be cells and cell clusters making up the living tissue of the community. That tissue, too, proves to be part of a larger organism—the world, whose inventions and visitations of the plague touch the lives of Middlemarchians.

The complexity of this unity can be seen in the very form Eliot's novels take. Though her works were long regarded as classic examples of the loose and baggy nineteenth-century novel, recent critics have found a unity in them which escaped earlier readers. Where Henry James found in *Middlemarch* a "treasurehouse of details" but an "indifferent whole," Barbara Hardy finds an intricate patterning of characters and events, of language and images. Interpreting form in a much wider sense, Hardy declares, "We are left with the impression, after reading one of her novels, that this is as close as the novelist can get to human multiplicity—that here form has been given to fluidity and expansiveness."[64]

From George Eliot's essay "Notes on Form in Art,"[65] we know her own ideas about structure. She began her discussion by showing how we arrive at a general notion of form by sorting out the relationship of parts to each other and to the whole. In fact, our concept of form is derived from the scientist who observes and organizes knowledge until "it arrives at the conception of wholes composed of parts more and more multiplied and highly differenced, yet more and more absolutely bound together by various conditions of common likeness or mutual dependence." Whether the object is a rock or a man, the Form is defined both by the intrinsic relation of its parts and by the outer play of forces upon it. And the "highest Form, then, is the highest organism, that is to say, the most varied group of relations bound together in a wholeness which again has the most varied relations with all other phenomena." "It is only in this fundamental sense," she added, "that the word Form can be applied to Art in general."

As for literature, Eliot's particular concern, "the choice and sequence of images and ideas—that is, of relations and groups of relations—are more or less not only determined by emotion but intended to express it. . . ." "*Poetry* [that is, literature] begins when passion weds thought by finding expression in an image"; but *Form* "begins in the choice of rhythms and images as signs of a mental state, for this is a process of grouping or association of a less spontaneous and more conscious order. . . ."

These reflections on Form, taken together with George Eliot's stated aim—to "enlarge the sympathies" and to stir "a more active admiration of those vital elements that bind men together"—take us back to Comte. On the one hand, there is the association with science, where Form is seen as the sorting out of the relationship of parts; on the other hand, there is the emotive origin of art, and with it the vitally expressive nature and conscious shaping of poetic image and structure. For Eliot as for Comte, the dissociation between intellect and emotion had to be resolved in a new synthesis, the kind of fusion embodied in poetic image and structure.

Despite her reservations about Positivism, George Eliot was obviously not as put off by the subjective method and by the *Système de politique positive* as were Lewes and Mill. And, though she could never accept Comte as the High Priest of her conscience and intellect, she could understand his political and social prescriptions as hypotheses.[66] It would seem that, for all her mistrust of any grandiose Key to all Mythologies, George Eliot perceived the creative nature of such syntheses. Just as she, as novelist, observed reality and wove the web of Middlemarchian relationships, the philosopher spins his much vaster synthesis.

In reality, is not her famous image of the pier glass, whose random scratches form themselves into concentric circles around a spot of light, a fit image for the subjective synthesis itself? Her tendency to move that spot of light distinguishes her from Comte. It has also disconcerted critics, who found themselves suddenly taken into the recesses of Casaubon's arid mind, for example. If by this device, her vivid picture of intellect gone dry (barely) escapes caricature, it does so by forcing us, for a moment at least, to contemplate the relationship of that exceedingly narrow spot of light to our own egoism. And, need we add, Eliot is also exposing the Comtean sins of intellect—narrow specialization, dryness, and pride. Thus Eliot's shift reminds us that this particular spot is also a scratch illuminated, in turn, by higher, brighter sources of light. Casaubon, only too human in his aspirations, is unable to cope with a universe that includes not only the idealistic Dorothea, but ancient mythologies, modern Germans, and Middlemarchian reality. He is measured against warm, vibrant human life and found wanting; he is measured against Past, Present, and Future and found wanting. That is, he is set in the context of that Higher Organism, all of Humanity and its evolving moral consciousness, and found wanting.

In Comte's synthesis, the ultimate light was precisely this moral knowledge; and what gave meaning to his universe was the moral progress of mankind, that developing sense of oneness, of interdependency. For Comte, the Highest Organism was complete in the great trinity: Humanity, Earth, and Space. For Eliot, the search was incomplete, and she continued to look for the Highest Organism and for the Highest Form.

As she searched, Eliot's imagination, like Lydgate's, found delight in "the exercise of disciplined power—combining and constructing with the clearest eye for probabilities and the fullest obedience to knowledge."[67] At this point in *Middlemarch*, the works of scientist, philosopher, and artist merge as in Comte's synthesis. The scientific imagination is deliberately set against the inadequacies of the romantic imagination. Yet the context also reminds us that the scientific imagination, too, can drift into dream and shipwreck. Though Eliot may seem close to Naturalism here, her emphasis is less on adapting scientific methodology than on the relationship of the poetic imagination to the great scientific powers of perception and coordination. To these, the poet adds the image and picture which clarify our conception of reality and which, through their emotive power, bring about "a more active admiration of those vital elements which bind men together and give a higher worthiness to their existence."

Thus Eliot's views regarding the poetic imagination and the functions of poetry are closely tied to Comte's philosophy. It was, however, the religious aspect of Positivism that drew her most strongly. Her religious temperament responded to the nobler side of the Religion of Humanity, even while she repudiated the narrow sectarianism of the Positivist Church. And, in the long run, *her* search for the Highest Organism and for the highest religion was open-ended: "I wish," she wrote to Clifford Allbutt, "you could thoroughly consider . . . whether it is probable that in a stage of society in which the ordinary standard of moral possibility, nay, of moral requirements, is still so low as I think you must recognize it to be, the highest possible religion has been evolved and accepted?"[68] In the openness of her meliorism, George Eliot reached beyond the Religion of Humanity.

CHAPTER 6

Conclusion

THE space of more than a century between us and Comte has done little to clarify his image. Now, the paradoxes of his own nature are overlaid with the multiple reflections, compounded of everything from firmly delineated parts to free-floating myth. We are challenged to define the impact on society of a man whose characteristics could be so negatively summed up as they are by Sir Isaiah Berlin: "His grotesque pedantry, the unreadable dullness of his writing, his vanity, his eccentricity, his solemnity, the pathos of his private life, his insane dogmatism, his authoritarianism, his philosophical fallacies. . . . [his] naïve craving for unity and symmetry at the expense of experience," his "bureaucratic fantasies . . . with his fanatically tidy world of human beings joyfully engaged in fulfilling their functions, each within his own rigorously defined province, in the rationally ordered, totally unalterable hierarchy of the perfect society."[1] As Simon observes, the fact that Comte's system had any diffusion at all is not something to be taken for granted. Given the weaknesses of his doctrines and the unattractiveness of his style, literary and personal, the critic cannot but wonder how Comte found any following at all. "That such a system so presented should have enlisted hundreds of full-fledged disciples and attracted partial assent from hundreds of others, including names both famous and unknown, is a matter that calls for explanation."[2] And the explanation has to encompass, too, the view that Comte might be regarded "as the central figure of his century—of the century whose special problem was the reconciling of destruction with reconstruction, negation with affirmation, science with religion, the head with the heart, the past with the present, order with progress."[3] Out of these multiple images how can we find the truest of all possible Comtes? Is the essential Comte the comprehensive systematizer of knowledge, the self-proclaimed Messiah of the Religion of Humanity, the organizer of the new sociocracy, or the Blakean angel—the visionary creator who tries to project his dream on us?

For many, the main contribution of Comte was his vast synthesis of all knowledge. Comte's comprehensiveness of view and vigor of mind represented to them the dawn of a new era—an era in which science and technology could be seen in proper perspective and put into integral relationship with the life of mankind.[4] Whether we view this synthesis as a philosophy, as a history of science, or as a philosophy of science, we see the same strengths—and the flaws that go with them. As systematizer, he could not rest until his system was complete—and rigid; every detail had to be made to fit into that closed structure. Nevertheless, Comte's history of science, his classification of the sciences, and his development of sociology all represent significant contributions to Western thought.[5]

In his moral and religious concepts, Comte was no less creative. On the one hand, his cultural relativism and his belief in moral progress attracted those who needed reassurance that mankind could develop spiritual values, even without the assistance of divine wisdom. Meliorism and creative evolution had strong roots here. On the other hand, Comte's Religion of Humanity appealed to those who needed an organized church. Unfortunately, that organization hardened into the same rigidity as his intellectual system; and, as Voegelin points out, the dangers implicit in Comte's spiritual dictatorship are not ones we can safely ignore.[6] Though we recoil from his authoritarianism, it was precisely this attempt to forge a new religion "that makes it possible," says Basil Willey, "to regard Comte as the central figure of his century. . . ."[7] It was here that he addressed himself to some of the most troubling issues of his day— and their source in the all too general spiritual disorientation.

Comte's moral and religious ideas were closely linked to his plans for the new sociocracy, and the main link between the two was education. Though Comte's specific course of instruction was not adopted, his work encouraged interest in education for all. The educational program he devised was progressive in its emphasis on the general principles of science and the broad outlines of history; though it was, perhaps, too oriented to science, too uniform, and too little encouraging to the free play of mind. Despite its scientific base, however, Comte's program bared the fact that education is, in reality, moral and social in nature; he clearly designed his educational system to manipulate public opinion.

As for the social structure that this public opinion was to recreate, it had its anomalies, too. Though Comte was on the side of the social planners, he at first expected the new society he envisioned to come about by a natural process of evolution. Ultimately, he simply awaited the arrival of the dictator who would imprint it on the world. Comte seems naive in his belief that a spiritual force would develop that would be strong enough to control either human greed or the increasingly threatening power of modern technology; he was sanguine enough to think that altruism could be effectively cultivated in a society built on competition (capitalism). Indeed, the morality that Comte enjoined taught submission to the powers that be and encouraged a passivity that would simply justify the status quo. The Brazilian novelist Machado de Assis neatly satirized this aspect of Comte's ideas in his portrait of Quincas Borba, the mad philosopher of Humanitism, whose motto is: To the winner the potatoes![8]

With Machado de Assis's challenging of the Comtean vision, we are reminded again of Blake's turning on the Angel who has almost imposed his vision of Hell on him. What strikes us most of all with Comte is the tenacious strength and unitary nature of his vision. Such intensity of vision tends to impose itself on others. The force of Comte's imagination seems to have made its impression, as we have seen, whether extolling the virtues of objectivity (or scientism), of utopianism, or of the subjective empire of Love.

George Eliot pictured just that intensity of vision in her portrait of Mordecai in *Daniel Deronda*—no matter that her "real model" was Emmanuel Deutsch.[9] Mordecai, poor and scorned, lives with an adoptive family; learned, he lives in and for a dream—a vision of the Jews restored to their land and reunited as a nation. This enthusiast feeds himself on visions, for, he says, "visions are the creators and feeders of the world. I see, I measure the world as it is, which the vision will create anew."[10]

So, too, was Comte absorbed by his vision of unification. His real life was marred by poverty, mental illness, and difficulties with family, wife, colleagues, and the establishment; but his system, he convinced himself, would make all into harmonious oneness. His dogged search for this unity—his idealization of relationships (his mother, Clotilde, Sophie)—his own almost-immaculate conception of the final synthesis (he did need some help from Clotilde)—these are Comte's steps into the world of vision. It is surely ironic that this man, whose name is for many synonymous with scientism, is at heart so thorough-going a Romantic.

The inevitable effect of such vision is, as Eliot says of Mordecai, the belief that this dream must have a farther destiny, fulfillment in reality. "An insane exaggeration of his own value, even if his ideas had been as true and precious as those of Columbus or Newton, many would have counted this yearning, taking it as the sublimer part for a man to say, 'If not I, then another,' and to hold cheap the meaning of his own life. But the fuller nature desires to be an agent, to create, and not merely to look on. . . . And while there is warmth enough in the sun to feed an energetic life, there will still be men to feel, 'I am lord of this moment's change, and will charge it with my soul.' "[11]

So, too, Comte sought to fulfill his destiny. Anointing himself High Priest of Humanity—as Napoleon had crowned himself Emperor—Comte saw himself as the spiritual leader not only of France but of the Republic of the West.

But Mordecai is not just a visionary, he is also a dying man. Aware that he himself will never fulfill his dream, he searches for the heir to whom he can entrust this sacred vision. The young man who has taken him into his family is too preoccupied with business; this young man's small son, though he loves Mordecai, only plays contentedly with a bright farthing while Mordecai is trying to plant in his young mind a sense of the spiritual richness of the Hebrew past, and to fire this young heart with his own glowing hopes for the future. Finally, Mordecai meets Daniel Deronda and sees in him the one he has been seeking. Though sympathetic, Daniel can only respond to Mordecai's vision of him as the reincarnation of himself: But I am not of your race. Eventually, however, Daniel discovers that he is a Jew. In finding his roots and his heritage (his blood, and the ancient manuscripts left him by his father), Daniel finds himself—and he accepts the dead hand of the Past, the present task, and the vision of Mordecai. "It is," Daniel says, "through your inspiration that I have discerned what may be my life's task. . . . Since I began to read and to know, I have always longed for some ideal task, in which I might feel myself the heart and brain of a multitude—some social captainship, which would come to me as a duty, and not be striven for as a personal prize." And Daniel makes the pledge of his life with "sacred solemnity."[12]

Mordecai's dream of the Jewish nation as the spiritual heart of mankind and of the restored Jewish nation as the unifier of East and West has lost some of its glow for us in the twentieth century. This heart seems as corrupt and divided as the rest of the world's body, and unification seems more beyond our capabilities than ever. History has an unpleasant way, as Voegelin points out, of turning dream into nightmare.

Comte found no son and heir, no High Priest he could anoint as his successor. For all that, there were those who accepted the heritage, the task, and the vision of Humanity's High Priest, and through that found the transmutation of the self that they, like Daniel, had yearned for. Comte's vision—whether it was that of Devil or Angel—was, indeed, a Memorable Fancy.

Notes and References

Chapter One

1. Letter to his friend A. Valat, November 16, 1825.
2. Henri Gouhier, *La vie d'Auguste Comte* (Paris, 1931), p. 9. Much of the material regarding Comte's life has been taken from this source, but two accounts by contemporaries of Comte—Emile Littré and Dr. J. F. E. Robinet—also provided useful information. Comte's letters and his own accounts of his life have also been used to a limited extent.
3. Jean François Eugène Robinet, *Notice sur l'oeuvre et sur la vie d'Auguste Comte* (Paris, 1891).
4. Emile Littré, *Auguste Comte et la philosophie positive* (Paris, 1863).
5. Gouhier, p. 48.
6. Ibid., p. 135. Also see *System of Positive Polity* (hereafter cited as *System*), III, xix, for Comte's view of Saint-Simon.
7. Comte wrote his Testament in 1855. It was published in 1884. The second edition (Paris, 1896) included *l'Addition secrète*.
8. Gouhier, p. 138.
9. Robinet, pp. 395–98.
10. J. S. Mill, with his friends M. Grote, Sir William Molesworth, and Raikes Currie, made up a subsidy to support Comte for a year.
11. This essay, published in 1865, was later revised and published in book form (London, 1866).
12. These articles from Littré's journal, the *National*, were later published with the title *De la philosophie positive* (Paris: Ladrange 1845).
13. For Comte's view of the utopias offered by communism and socialism see *System*, I, 120–36.
14. In the *Préface Personelle* to the last volume of the *Cours* (1842), Comte tells us that for the last twenty years he had refused to read any literature that dealt with the subject he was working on, for he wanted to preserve the integrity *(l'esprit fondamental)* of his work. Gouhier dates from 1838 Comte's abstention from reading.
15. Gouhier, pp. 282–83.
16. For Comte's discussion of Vico (1668–1744) see *System*, III, 504.
17. For Comte's discussion of Montesquieu (1689–1755) see Harriet Martineau (hereafter cited as HM), 442–44, *System*, III, 504; IV, 568–70, 603.
18. Turgot (1727–1821), *Historical Progress* (1749). See *System*, III, 499–502.
19. Condorcet (1743–1794), *Esquisse* (1793). See HM, 444–45; *System*, IV, 570–80.

20. Keith Mitchell Baker, *Condorcet* (Chicago, 1975).

21. For a discussion of Burdin's extension of scientific methodology to physiology and his influence on Comte, see Littré on the background of Comte's philosophy. See also Robinet, p. 112; Gouhier, *Vie*, p. 19, and *Jeunesse d'Auguste Comte*, III, 396–400. This quotation is from Saint-Simon, *Mémoire* (Brussels, 1859), pp. 21–24.

22. Joseph de Maistre (1754–1821), *Du Pape* (1817). See *System*, III, 519, 527–28; IV, 631–32.

23. Babeuf (1760–1797), political agitator and early propounder of Socialism.

24. Fourier (1772–1837), socialist noted for his community plan based on the phalanstère.

25. Robinet, p. 117.

26. For a record of the publication of this work and the break between Comte and Saint-Simon, see Gouhier, *Jeunesse*, III, ch. VII. See also Comte's attacks on Saint-Simon in *Cours de philosophie positive* (hereafter cited as *Cours*), VI, *Preface Personelle; System*, III, Preface.

Chapter Two

1. All references will be to the English translation, *System of Positive Polity* (London, 1875–1877), and will be indicated in the text by volume and page number.

2. Cabanis (1757–1808). See HM, 369–98 for Comte's discussion of the work of Cabanis, Bichat, and Gall in the development of physiology. See also *System*, I, 459–594; IV, 581.

3. *Lettres d'Auguste Comte à M. Valat, professeur de mathématiques* (Paris, 1870), p. 38. The letter is dated April 17, 1818.

4. Broussais (1772–1838).

5. Comte's views regarding the introspective method are called an aberration by J. S. Mill, *Auguste Comte and Positivism* (Ann Arbor, 1965), pp. 63–67.

6. Gall (1758–1828) was a physician and phrenologist. While Comte accepted the basic idea of phrenology, he proceeded, characteristically, to correct Gall's map of the brain.

Chapter Three

1. The references to the *Course* will be found in the abridged English translation by Harriet Martineau (New York, 1974—two volumes in one) and will be indicated in the text by HM and the page number. Comte himself so approved of Martineau's abridged edition that he substituted it for his own six-volume edition in the Positivist Library.

2. The classification of elements is systematized by the work of Lothar Meyer and D. I. Mendeléyev on the "periodic laws" (1860s to 1880s).

3. Mill, p. 53.

4. Herbert Spencer, *Reasons for Dissenting from the Philosophy of M. Comte* (Berkeley, 1968), pp. 10, 15.

5. Mill, pp. 106–18.

6. Ibid., pp. 61–62.

7. Comte, *Cours de philosophie positive*, VI, 639–47.

8. Mill, pp. 61–62.

9. Eric Voegelin, *From Enlightenment to Revolution* (Durham, N.C., 1975), p. 150. See also Pierre Ducassé, *Méthode et intuition chez Auguste Comte* (Paris, 1939), and also F. S. Marvin, *Comte, the Founder of Sociology* (New York, 1937), who sees Comte's work as an aesthetic structure rather than as empirical science.

10. This interpretation is that of Eric Voegelin, chs. VI and VII, especially pp. 158, 166.

Chapter Four

1. The references to the *System of Positive Polity* will be to the English translation and will be indicated in the text by *System* and volume and page number.

2. Gouhier, *Vie*, pp. 228–42.

3. Voegelin, pp. 161–66.

4. See *System*, III, Appendix to the Preface.

5. Comte's hypothesis is that the purity of women will evolve still more, so that eventually they will be independent of men so far as reproduction is concerned. See, for example, *System* IV, 60–61, 241–42. Parthogenesis is only one of Comte's strange ideas.

6. Comte does, at least in the *General View*, make allowance for exceptional women. His example is Joan of Arc, whose military calling could be accommodated by Positivism, even though it is an anomaly. *System*, I, 212–14.

7. The proletariat, for Comte, meant the working people as contrasted with the middle class and the capitalists. The middle-class people may work, but they are regarded by Comte as parasitic and useless.

8. Though hostile to Napoleon in his youth, Comte later seemed to imitate his program for unifying the West and Russia under French leadership. See Voegelin, pp. 168–70, for an analysis of this relationship.

9. New York, 1968.

10. Aron, pp. 89–91.

11. Simon, p. 46.

12. Aron, p. 123.

13. Voegelin, p. 90.

14. Ibid., p. 158.

15. Aron, pp. 123–24.

16. Voegelin, p. 159.

Chapter Five

1. See *System,* I, 225, and IV, General Appendix, 551, for Comte's views regarding the subordination of imagination to intellect. Comte's impatience with the established academic training can be seen, for example, in *System,* I, 246–47.

2. See also *System,* I, 233; II, ch. IV, "The Positive Theory of Languge." Comte develops Diderot's theory of language in this section of *System,* II.

3. See, for example, HM, pp. 568–70, 632, 836–37.

4. W. M. Simon calls Comte's "a German *esprit de système*, producing a *système* with absolutely no *esprit* at all" (p. 9).

5. Comte's festival idea resembles the vast *Gesamtkunstwerk* proposed by Wagner. Comte's proposal for a Universal Language is found in *System,* II, 220, 382; IV, 66–67, 85, 419. Comte believed that Italian would be the logical choice for this universal language.

6. Comte imagined himself as writing in 1927, by which time Positivism would be well established (Preface, p. viii). Except as otherwise indicated, references in this part are to the *Synthèse subjective* (Paris, 1856; reprint Brussels, 1969.)

7. This emphasis on intellect's pride and dryness is somewhat odd in a work on Positivist logic; but in this treatise Comte is more interested in the adaptation of the subjective methodology than he is in the subject matter.

8. "Ne devant jamais aspirer aux notions absolues, nous pouvons instituer la conception relative des corps extérieurs en douant chacun d'eux des facultés de sentir et d'agir, pourvu que nous leur ôtions la pensée, en sorte que leurs volontés soient toujours aveugles" (p. 8). ("Unable ever to aspire to absolute ideas, we can begin our conceptualization of external nature by attributing to all things the faculties of feeling and acting, providing that we take thought away from them since their wills are always blind.")

9. "Tous les chefs-d'oeuvre poétiques font directement ressortir la partie supérieure de la méthode universelle, en subordonnant la déduction et l'induction à la construction . . ." (pp. 43–44). ("All poetic masterpieces make the superiority of the universal method stand out, because they subordinate deduction and induction to construction.")

10. "Le concours normal des sentiments, des images, et des signes, pour nous inspirer les conceptions qui conviennent à nos besoins, moraux, intellectuels, et physiques" vs. the old logic which "se borne à nous *dévoiler* les vérités qui nous conviennent . . ." (p. 27).

11. Comte complained that conventional logic limited itself to deduction and induction "comme si le domaine fictif n'existait pas pour nous, ou ne comportait aucune règle" (p. 27). (". . . as if the domain of fiction did not exist for us, or did not have any rules.")

12. "Nous devons autant systematizer la conjecture que la démonstration . . ." (p. 27). ("We ought to systematize conjecture as much as demonstration. . . .")

13. "[La logique religieuse] doit être finalement complêté par le domaine, beaucoup plus vaste et non moins légitime, des conceptions propres à développer le sentiment sans'choquer la raison" (p. 40).

14. That is, any hypothesis has to satisfy three conditions for Comte: it must not contradict known facts; it must be logically coherent; and it must, above all, contribute to Humanity's well-being.

15. Mill, pp. 61–62.

16. Earth, the Grand-Fétiche, may be imagined as having had intelligence at one time, though it exhausted that intelligence in its work of preparing itself for Humanity's existence (p. 10).

17. See pp. 18–19, 24 for Comte's description of Space, the Grand Milieu.

18. For example, "le triumvirat qui résume la synthèse subjective doit universellement développer les habitudes vraiment organiques en faisant directement apprécier la soumission comme la base de toute harmonie . . ." (p. 53). See also pp. 17–19, 35, 37. ("The triumvirate which represents the totality of the subjective synthesis ought to universally develop truly organic habits by making it directly understood that submission is the basis of all harmony.")

19. ". . . Il faut . . . que le commandement assiste l'arrangement, afin que l'*ordre* soit complet" (p. 25).

20. "A la poésie seule appartient ensuite de faire assez sentir la principale efficacité des institutions destinées à généraliser le type humain en y rattachant, autant que possible, la matière et même l'espace" (p. 26). (It belongs to poetry alone to make sufficiently felt the principal efficacity of the institutions destined to generalize the human type by drawing matter, and even space, close to it, as much as possible.")

21. See Louis Martz, *The Meditative Poem* (New York: *Doubleday*, 1963), pp. xix, 11–13.

22. Ibid., p. xxiii.

23. Comte explains the plan he has "finalement institué pur toutes les compositions importantes . . ." (pp. 755–61). (". . . finally instituted for all important compositions. . . .")

24. "Formé de deux progressions suivies d'une synthèse, ou d'une progression entre deux couples, le nombre sept, succédant à la somme des trois nombres sacrés, détermine le plus vaste groupe que nous puissions distinctement imaginer. Réciproquement, il pose la limite des divisions que nous pouvons directement concevoir dans une grandeur quelconque" (p. 127).

25. "Normalement formée, la section offre un groupe central de sept phrases, que précèdent et suivent trois groupes de cinq: la section initiale de chaque partie réduit à trois phrases trois de ses groupes symétriquement

placés: la section finale donne sept phrases à chacun des groupes extrêmes"
(p. 755).

26. "L'impression phonique complète l'effet graphique" (p. 757).

27. In bringing together philosophy and poetry in this work, Comte tells
us, he has realized "combien le perfectionnement de l'intelligence, comme
celui du sentiment et de l'activité, repose sur une digne soumission" (p.
xiv).

28. "Il importe à l'harmonie sociale que les meilleures formes de la
composition, philosophique ou poétique, l'interdise aux médiocrités, et la
rende même exceptionelle chez les âmes d'élite . . ." (p. 761).

29. See Edward Dawson's description of meditation as "a diligent and
forcible application of the understanding, to seeke, and knowe, and as it
were to tast some divine matter; from whence doth arise in our affectionate
powers good motions, inclinations, and purposes which stirre us up to the
love and exercise of vertue. . . ." Martz, p. 3.

30. This discussion will be limited to literature, partly because of the
limitations of space, but also because Comte dealt most with literature.

31. Emile Zola (1840–1902) propounded his literary theory in "The Experimental Novel" and in "Naturalism in the Theatre." References following
are to these works as found in *Documents of Modern Literary Realism*,
George Joseph Becker, ed. (Princeton, 1963).

32. Claude Bernard (1813–1878) French physiologist, wrote *Introduction à la médecine expérimentale* (1865).

33. Claude Bernard's knowledge of Comte's work is discussed by Simon,
pp. 114–16.

34. Zola, "The Experimental Novel," *Documents*, pp. 167, 174.

35. Ibid., pp. 166–67.

36. "Naturalism in the Theatre," *Documents*, p. 208.

37. Ibid., p. 210.

38. See, for example, *System*, I, 232, for Comte's views of imitation. Art
cannot simply imitate, claims Comte, for even its closest copies of reality
aim at "construction" and "synthesis," and thus instigate change. Within
the negative context of the times, Comte claimed, "there has only been
left one service, of great temporary importance, for Art to render; the
idealization of doubt itself" (*System*, I, 239). See this whole section, *System*,
I, 239–56.

39. Edward Bellamy (1850–1898) is the American social reformer who
wrote *Looking Backward*, a popular and influential Utopian novel.

40. George Bernard Shaw (1856–1950) came under the influence of
Henry George in 1882 and became, in 1884, a member of the Fabian
Society.

41. For Bellamy's "Religion of Solidarity," see Joseph Schiffman, ed.,
Edward Bellamy: Selected Writings on Religion and Society (New York,
1955), pp. 3–57.

42. Bellamy also reflects Comtean ideas in his views on women, eugenics, and certain minor points.

43. See Schiffman, p. xxxix.

44. See Sylvia Bowman, *Edward Bellamy Abroad* (New York, 1962), p. 65.

45. Ibid. Bellamy's aim was to provide an environment promoting the cooperative rather than the competitive spirit.

46. The Marxists used parts of Bellamy's works—for example, "The Parable of the Water Tank"—even though Bellamy explicitly dissociated himself from the Socialists and Communists. See Bowman, pp. 33–37, 166.

47. See Schiffman, p. xxxv.

48. See Bowman, ch. I.

49. The Fabian Society was a Socialist organization founded in 1883–1884. In 1889 the society published *Fabian Essays*, the exposition of their evolutionary socialism. Chief among the members of this society were E. R. Pease, Sidney and Beatrice Webb, Annie Besant, and Shaw. For discussions of the relationship between Comte and Fabianism, see Willard Wolfe, *From Radicalism to Socialism* (New Haven, 1975), and Norman and Jeanne MacKenzie, *The Fabians* (New York, 1977).

50. For a discussion of Comtean ideas as adapted by Shaw, see Julian B. Kaye, *Bernard Shaw and the Nineteenth-Century Tradition* (Norman, Oklahoma, 1958).

51. Kaye notes that *Major Barbara* is "a critique of Comtianism" even while Undershaft's capitalism is a notable advance for society (p. 145).

52. Though Shaw was more concerned with economics than Comte was, Shaw's preface to *Major Barbara* deals with the moral obligation to work, the need for society to provide essentials for all, and the lack of a cohesive faith in modern society. Even Shaw's belief in Creative Evolution (closer to Lamarck than to Darwin, as Shaw himself points out) seems not far removed from Comte's belief in Humanity as perfecting itself. Shaw's belief in the vitality and spiritual force of woman also follows Comte.

53. Our concern here is not the extent of George Eliot's commitment to Positivism, but the way Positivist ideas are transformed in fiction. At any rate, contact with Comtean ideas—through her work on the *Westminster Review*, her liaison with George Henry Lewes, her friendship with Harrison and the Congreves—continued throughout most of her life.

54. Simon, pp. 210–11. See also Gordon S. Haight, *George Eliot* (New York, 1968), pp. 302, 405.

55. Letter to Frederic Harrison, August 15, 1866. This is reprinted in the Norton Critical Edition of *Middlemarch* (New York, 1977), pp. 593–94. All references to *Middlemarch* will be from this edition.

56. *Daniel Deronda* (1876). All references will be to the following edition: New York, 1900.

57. Letter to Clifford Allbutt, August 1868, in *Middlemarch*, p. 594.

58. Ibid.

59. Excerpt from *Adam Bede;* see *Middlemarch,* p. 588.

60. Letter to Charles Bray, July 5, 1859, in *Middlemarch,* p. 591.

61. Notes on *The Spanish Gypsy* (1868). On seeing an *Annunciation* by Titian, Eliot says, "it occurrred to me that here was a great dramatic motive. . . . A young maiden, believing herself to be on the eve of the chief event of her life—marriage— . . . has suddenly announced to her that she is chosen to fulfil a great destiny, entailing a terribly different experience from that of ordinary womanhood." And, Eliot adds, "I required the opposition of race to give the need for renouncing the expectation of marriage." Haight, p. 376.

62. Mordecai's (and Daniel's) vision is that Israel may establish its land and its polity, and that in the dignity of this national life Judaism may so plant the wisdom and skill of the race so that it may be, as of old, a medium of transmission and understanding (*Daniel Deronda,* II, 536). See also pp. 502–504, 530, 536–38, 541–42.

63. This passage continues: "Lydgate was aware that his concessions to Rosamond were often little more than the lapse of slackening resolution, the creeping paralysis apt to seize an enthusiasm which is out of adjustment to a constant portion of our lives" (*Middlemarch,* p. 405).

64. Barbara Hardy, *The Novels of George Eliot* (New York, 1959), p. 238.

65. "Notes on Form" (1868) in *Middlemarch,* pp. 595–97.

66. Haight, p. 390.

67. This passage begins with Lydgate's delight in the labor of the scientific imagination, and this kind of creativity is set beside the gift of "profuseness in indifferent drawing or cheap narration." Lydgate rather arrogantly dismisses that kind of invention as "diseased," "vulgar and vinous," and cheap because it projects romantic scenes and people rather than reality. The irony is, of course, that his own dream is a romantic one— as Eliot skillfully shows us in the rosy, floating daydream which follows (*Middlemarch,* pp. 113–14).

68. Letter to Clifford Allbutt, August 1868, in *Middlemarch,* p. 595.

Chapter Six

1. Isaiah Berlin, *Historical Inevitability* (London, 1954), pp. 4–5, 22; and *The Hedgehog and the Fox* (New York: Mentor, 1957), p. 26.

2. Simon, pp. 8–9.

3. Willey, p. 188.

4. George Henry Lewes, *History of Philosophy from Thales to Comte* (London, 1880), vol. II, p. 690.

5. See, for example, Simon, p. 269.

6. See above, pp. 123–126.

7. Willey, p. 188.

8. Machado de Assis (1839–1908), *Quincas Borba* (Rio, 1891). Machado de Assis's revolt against Positivism is of particular interest because it was in Brazil that Comte's influence reached farthest into the realm of practical politics and lingered longest. The republic that took shape in 1891 (after the downfall of the Empire in 1889) borrowed some of its ideology from Comte and found its practical model in the American constitution. *Ordem e Progresso* [Order and Progress], the republic's motto, is still to be seen on the Brazilian flag. Positivist religion found loyal followers in Brazil, and its rituals were observed in Positivist temples. See João Cruz Costa, *A History of Ideas in Brazil* (Berkeley, 1964), for a discussion of Positivist influence in Brazil. The Humanitism of Quincas Borba (and of his heir, Rubião) demonstrates the use of a fine-sounding name to mask the egoism at the heart of this philosophy. Just as Comte had "justified" war and shown its benefits to progressing mankind, Borba "justifies" avarice, envy, disease, and war. Borba illustrates the benefits of war in his parable of two starving tribes battling over a field of potatoes. Were they to divide the crop peacefully, both tribes would be decimated by starvation. By fighting till one tribe is exterminated, they ensure that one tribe at least will flourish—"To the victor the potatoes." See Helen Caldwell, *Machado de Assis* (Berkeley, 1970), pp. 89–90, 112–13, for her discussion of Positivism in *Memórias Posthumas de Braz Cubas* (Rio, 1881) and *Quincas Borba*, the novels in which Borba plays an important part.

9. See Haight, p. 469. Also see Hardy, pp. 108–14. Hardy makes the important point that Eliot is not simply idealizing the Jew but drawing parallels between Jew and Gentile.

10. *Daniel Deronda*, II, 502.

11. Ibid., p. 479.

12. Ibid., p. 755.

Selected Bibliography

PRIMARY SOURCES

1. Major works by Auguste Comte
Cours de philosophie positive. 6 vols. Paris: Bachelier, 1830–1842.
Cours de philosophie positive. 3rd ed. with preface by Emile Littré. 6 vols.
   Paris: J. B. Baillière, 1869.
Synthèse subjective. Paris: L'auteur, 1856; rpt. Bruxelles: Culture et Civ-
   ilisation, 1969.
Système de politique positive. 4 vols. Paris: Imp. Larousse, 1879–1893.

2. Miscellaneous Writings
Appel aux conservateurs. Paris: L'auteur, V. Dalmont, 1855.
Calendrier positiviste. Paris: L. Mathias, 1849; rpt. Bruxelles: Culture et
   Civilisation, 1969.
Catéchisme positiviste. Ed. Pierre Arnaud. Paris: Garnier-Flammarion,
   1966.
Correspondance inédite. 4 vols. Paris: Société Positiviste, 1903–1904.
Discours sur l'ensemble du positivisme. Paris: L. Mathias, 1848.
Lettres d'Auguste Comte à John Stuart Mill. Paris: E. Leroux, 1877.
Lettres d'Auguste Comte à M. Valat. Paris: Dunod, 1870.
Testament d'Auguste Comte. Paris: 1896.

3. English Translations
A General View of Positivism. Tr. J. H. Bridges. London: Trübner & Co.,
   1865; rpt. Stanford, California: Academic Reprints, n.d.
The Positive Philosophy. Tr. and condensed by Harriet Martineau. New
   York: C. Blanchard, 1855; rpt. (2 vols. in one) New York: AMS Press,
   1979.
System of Positive Polity, Tr. by J. H. Bridges, F. Harrison, E. S. Beesly,
   R. Congreve, and others. 4 vols. London: Longmans, Green and Com-
   pany, 1875–1877.

SECONDARY SOURCES

1. Books
ARNAUD, PIERRE. *La Pensée d'August Comte*. Paris: Bordas, 1969.
———. *Politique d'Auguste Comte*. Selected texts and commentary by
   Pierre Arnaud. Paris: A. Colin, 1965. An able presentation of Comte's
   basic ideas by one who thinks that Comte's work in its entirety ought
   to be better known.

ARON, RAYMOND. *Main Currents in Sociological Thought*. Tr. Richard Howard and Helen Weaver. New York: Anchor Books, 1968. I, 73–143. This chapter provides a valuable summary of Comte's sociological ideas, and the book as a whole deals with other main figures—Montesquieu, Marx, and Tocqueville—in the history of sociology.

BAKER, KEITH MITCHELL. *Condorcet*. Chicago: University of Chicago Press, 1975. A fine analysis of Condorcet's work and of his place in the history of social science.

BECKER, GEORGE JOSEPH, ed. *Documents of Modern Literary Realism*. Princeton: Princeton University Press, 1963. A useful reference book for both Realism and Naturalism.

BELLAMY, EDWARD. *Looking Backward*. Boston: Houghton Mifflin, 1941. A utopian novel with many Positivist elements.

BERLIN, ISAIAH. *Historical Inevitability*. London: Oxford University Press, 1954. A general study of determinism and its implications when applied to the interpretation of history.

BOWMAN, SYLVIA. *Edward Bellamy Abroad*. New York: Twayne, 1962. A valuable reference source.

CALDWELL, HELEN. *Machado de Assis*. Berkeley: University of California Press, 1970. A useful study of his work and of various influences on his work, including Positivism.

COSTA, JOÃO CRUZ. *A History of Ideas in Brazil*. Tr. Suzette Macedo. Berkeley: University of California Press, 1964. A valuable source of information about the influence of Positivism in Brazil.

CRESSON, ANDRÉ. *Auguste Comte*. Paris: Presses universitaires de France, 1957. A brief treatment of Comte's life and work.

DUCASSÉ, PIERRE. *Méthode et intuition chez Auguste Comte*. Paris: F. Alcan, 1939. An interesting and valuable study of Comtean intuition.

DUMAS, GEORGES. *Psychologie de Deux Messies Positivistes: Saint-Simon et Auguste Comte*. Paris: F. Alcan, 1905. An interesting study of the Messianic complex in these two men.

DURKHEIM, EMILE. *Socialism and Saint-Simon*. Ed. Alvin W. Gouldner and tr. Charlotte Sattler. Ohio: Antioch Press, 1958. Informative discussion of Saint-Simon's work and of the social and industrial background.

ELIOT, GEORGE. *Daniel Deronda*. 2 vols.; *Felix Holt; The Spanish Gypsy*. New York: E. R. Dumont, 1900 (Little, Brown).

———. *Middlemarch*. Ed. Bert G. Hornback. (Norton Critical Edition.) New York: Norton, 1977.

GOUHIER, HENRI G. *La jeunesse d'Auguste Comte*. 3 vols. Paris: J. Vrin, 1933–1941.

———. *La vie d'Auguste Comte*. Paris: Gallimard, 1931. The best works on Comte's life and the development of his thought.

HAIGHT, GORDON S. *George Eliot*. New York: Oxford University Press, 1968. A good modern biography of Eliot which refers briefly to her contact with Positivism.

HARDY, BARBARA. *The Novels of George Eliot*. New York: Oxford University Press, 1959. Some mention of Positivism.

KAYE, JULIAN B. *Bernard Shaw and the Nineteenth Century Tradition*. Norman, Oklahoma: University of Oklahoma Press, 1958. Shaw's indebtedness to several nineteenth-century thinkers, including Comte.

LÉVY-BRUHL, LUCIEN. *La philosophie d'Auguste Comte*. 4th ed. Paris: F. Alcan, 1921. A sympathetic treatment of Comte's work.

LEWES, GEORGE HENRY. *Comte's Philosophy of the Sciences*. London: G. Bell and Sons, 1883. An explication of Comte's philosophy of science.

————. *The History of Philosophy from Thales to Comte*. 5th ed. Vol. II. London: Longmans, Green and Company, 1880. A very favorable evaluation of Comte's contributions to the history of science.

LITTRÉ, EMILE. *Auguste Comte et la philosophie positive*. Paris: Hachette, 1863. An interesting and useful source from the point of view of the "intellectual Positivists."

MACHADO DE ASSIS, JOAQUIM MARIA. *Memorias Posthumas de Braz Cubas*. Rio: Instituto Nacional do Livro, 1960.

————. *Quincas Borba*. Rio: W. M. Jackson, 1957.

MACKENZIE, NORMAN and JEANNE. *The Fabians*. New York: Simon and Schuster, 1977. An excellent study of this Socialist movement and its indebtedness to Comte.

MARCUSE, HERBERT. "The Positive Philosophy of Society: Auguste Comte" in *Reason and Revolution*. 2nd ed. New York: Humanities Press, 1954. A study primarily of Hegel and Hegelianism, which deals with Comte's Positivism as a reaction against "critical rationalism," and as a philosophic system which encourages too much submission to the given.

MARVIN. F. S. *Comte, The Founder of Sociology*. New York: Wiley and Sons, 1937. A somewhat older study from the point of view of a Positivist interested in Comte's contributions to history and sociology.

MILL, JOHN STUART. *Auguste Comte and Positivism*. Ann Arbor: University of Michigan Press, 1965. Mill's brief survey of Positivism is somewhat limited but useful in showing Mill's appreciation of and reservations about Positivism.

ROBINET, J. F. E. *Notice sur l'oeuvre et sur la vie d'Auguste Comte*. 3rd ed. Paris: Soc. Positiviste, 1891. Comte's life and work defended as an integral whole by a dedicated disciple—anti-Littréist, anti–Mme. Comte.

SAINT-SIMON, CLAUDE HENRI, COMTE DE. *Mémoire sur la science de l'homme*, in *Oeuvres choisis*, II. Bruxelles: F. Van Meenen, 1859. Of interest for relation of Comte's general background.

SCHIFFMAN, JOSEPH, ed. *Edward Bellamy: Selected Writings on Religion and Society*. New York: Liberal Arts Press, 1955. Only brief reference to Comte.

SHAW, GEORGE BERNARD. *Major Barbara*. Baltimore: Penguin, 1967. A play with many Positivist elements.

SIMON, W. M. *European Positivism in the Nineteenth Century*. Ithaca, N.Y.: Cornell University Press, 1963. An excellent study of Positivist influence—a model of thoroughness.

SPENCER, HERBERT. *Reasons for Dissenting from the Philosophy of M. Comte*. Berkeley, California: Glendessary Press, 1968. Spencer's objections to Positivism.

VOEGELIN, ERIC. *From Enlightenment to Revolution*. Ed. John H. Hallowell. Durham, N.C.: Duke University Press, 1975. A thorough analysis of Comte's religion and its apocalyptic nature.

WILLEY, BASIL. *Nineteenth Century Studies*. New York: Harper and Row, 1949; rpt. Harper Torchbooks, 1966. A standard study in the intellectual background of the period.

WOLFE, WILLARD. *From Radicalism to Socialism*. New Haven: Yale University Press, 1975. A useful study of Fabian socialism and of Comtean influence on the Fabians.

2. Articles

ARBOUSSE-BASTIDE, PAUL. "Auguste Comte et la sociologie religieuse." *Archives de Sociologie des Religions* 11: 22 (July-December 1966): 3–58. Claims that Comte's contribution to the sociology of religion was minimal, yet his thought suggests important lines of investigation.

ARNAUD, PIERRE. "La 'Maladie Occidentale.' Un diagnostic toujours actuel d'Auguste Comte." *L'Année Sociologique* 23 (1972) (troisième série): 9–70. Presents the fundamentals of Comte's approach to sociology and shows the relevance of this approach in the light of today's problems.

BRYANT, CHRISTOPHER G. A. "Positivism Reconsidered." *Sociological Review* 23: 2 (May 1975): 395–412. Discriminates between Comtean and instrumental positivism. (The latter refers to quantitative, empirical research methods.)

BULLEN, J. B. "George Eliot's *Romola* as a Positivist Allegory." *Review of English Studies* ns 26: 104 (November 1975): 425–35. Deals with *Romola* as echoing Positivist ideas and as exemplifying the educative value of history as a record of mankind's spiritual evolution.

COHEN, D. "Comte's Changing Sociology." *American Journal of Sociology* 71 (Summer 1965): 168–77. Exposes as erroneous the idea that Comte's contribution to sociology was the scientific approach to social data, since Comte shifted from that approach to a quest for the grounds of social solidarity.

DEGRANGE, MCQUILKIN. "Comte's Sociologies." *American Sociological Review* 4: 1 (February 1939): 17–26. Deals with Comte's gradual redefinition of sociology and its relationship with psychology. Predicts increasing respect for Comte as a creative thinker, particularly as Comte's later works are more studied.

FARMER, MARY E. "The Positivist Movement and the Development of English Sociology," *Sociological Review* 15 (May 1967): 5–20. Discusses Positivism as a direct influence on the first generation of English sociologists, but then as less important when there set in a reaction in the other direction (emphasis on statistical method and more rigorous discipline). Need to reevaluate the foundations of sociology.

FOUST, LINDA F. "Auguste Comte, the Father of Sociology: His Perspective on Methodology and the Discipline Today." Paper for the Annual Meeting of the Southern Sociological Society, 1978. Holds that a study of recent methodological texts shows a distinct divergence from Comte's methodology.

GIDDENS, ANTHONY. "The High Priest of Positivism." *Times Literary Supplement,* 14 November 1975, pp. 1359–60. A discussion of Comte's work in connection with the publication of a new two-volume French edition of the *Cours*. Remarks on the inadequacies of Comtean sociology (and its reworking by Durkheim) and of Comtean Positivism (and its radical, Vienna-circle form).

GOLLIN, GILLIAN LINDT. "Theories of the Good Society: Four Views on Religion and Social Change," *Journal for the Scientific Study of Religion* 9: 1 (Spring 1970): 1–16. A comparative analysis of the sociological theories of religion of Saint-Simon, Comte, Proudhon, and Marx.

GROSS, D. H. "Browning's Positivist Count in Search of a Miracle: A Grim Parody in *The Ring and the Book.*" *Victorian Poetry* 12 (Summer 1974): 178–80. An interpretation of Guido as a grim parody of the rigorous materialist and positivist, and as an example of the consequences of rejecting the idea of moral values and of the soul.

LAFFEY, J. F. "Auguste Comte: Prophet of Reconciliation and Reaction." *Science and Society* 29 (Winter 1965): 44–65. Claims that Comte's work is a combination of revolutionary and reactionary ideas; but his synthesis is weighted socially and politically toward Reaction.

LAUDAN, LARRY. "Towards a Reassessment of Comte's 'Méthode Positive,' " *Philosophy of Science* 38: 1 (March 1971): 35–53. Affirms the importance of Comte's Positivism and claims that his theory of scientific method needs to be analyzed more carefully.

McALEER, EDWARD C. "Browning's 'Cleon' and Auguste Comte." *Comparative Literature* 8 (Spring 1956): 142–45. Interprets "Cleon" as Browning's discussion (and rejection) of Comte's concepts of the Great Being and of subjective immortality, and as Browning's defense of the Hebraic-Christian tradition.

MIDDLETON, RUSSELL. "A Reappraisal of Comte's Position in the Development of Sociology." *Sociology and Social Research* 44: 3 (January-February 1960): 178–84. An attempt to sort out Comte's real contributions to sociology and to correct misevaluation of Comte. Claims that Comte had little direct influence on the development of sociology, but enormous indirect influence through Durkheim.

MONTANARI, F. ORSELLO. "L'Idea di 'Umanità' Quale Elements di Sintesi del Sistema Comtiano." *Revista di Sociologia* 18: 2 (March-August 1970): 81–110. Unity as the fundamental concern of Comte's work.

MORAIS FILHO, EVARISTO DE. "A Sociologia do Jovem Comte, II." *Sociologia* 17: 4 (October 1955): 371–422. Stresses the centrality of the early works to Comte's thought and the timeliness of the basic premises and methodology there established.

ROGGERO, ELIO. "L'Attualità di Auguste Comte." *Critica Sociologica* 23 (Fall 1972): 134–50. A review of Comte's life and ideas which stresses various aspects of Positivism relevant today.

SAMELSON, FRANZ. "History, Origin Myth and Ideology: Comte's 'Discovery' of Social Psychology." *Journal for the Theory of Social Behaviour* 4: 2 (October 1974): 217–31. Argues that the history of psychology has been too concerned with "origin myths" and not enough concerned with critical historical analysis. Analysis of Comte's Positivism—e.g., shows it to be highly ideological and suggests questions about why these aspects were forgotten—and the role that unrecognized ideology plays in recent social psychology.

SCOTT, JAMES F. "George Eliot, Positivism, and the Social Vision of *Middlemarch.*" *Victorian Studies* 16: 1 (September 1972): 59–76. Deals with *Middlemarch* as depicting Comtean ideas (the moral-social disintegration, the failure of the Protestant Church and the aristocracy to provide leadership) and anti-Comtean ones (the abortive attempt of the new capitalist and new scientist to create the leadership needed for a new society). Argues, curiously, that Eliot's emphasis on the weight of the past and her placing of hope for the future in Dorothea's maternal hands are anti-Comtean.

SELLARS, ROY WOOD. "Positivism in Contemporary Philosophical Thought." *American Sociological Review* 4:1 (February 1939): 26–42. Traces the evolution of Positivism from Comte through the Vienna school and perceives as a major problem the Positivists' disregard of epistemology (the development of linguistics not an adequate substitute).

SIMON, W. M. "The 'Two Cultures' in Nineteenth-Century France: Victor Cousin and Auguste Comte." *Journal of the History of Ideas* 26: 1 (January-March 1965): 45–58. Claims that the antagonisms between Cousin and Comte created the mistaken view that there were two and only two antagonistic cultures (materialism and spiritualism). In fact, there were not two "cultures," but only one, with many streams.

SWINGEWOOD, ALAN. "Comte, Marx, and Political Economy." *Sociological Review* 18 (November 1970): 335–50. Examines Comte's relationship to eighteenth- and nineteenth-century political economy. Propounds the theory that Comte's treatment of social institutions and social change came from his misunderstanding of political economy.

VAN PATTEN, JAMES J. "A Religion of Humanity: Auguste Comte—Love, Order, Progress." *Revista Internacional de Sociologie* 31: 5–6 (January-June 1973): 1–19. Analysis of Comte's humanism as a way of achieving social reform at a minimum cost.

VERNON, RICHARD. "Auguste Comte and 'Development': A Note." *History and Theory* 17: 3 (1978): 323–26. Discusses three different "designs" in Comte's tracing of the development of human events. In all three, however, secularization is presented as a crucial part of historical development.

WARD, J. P. "Wordsworth and the Sociological Idea." *Critical Quarterly* 16 (Winter 1974): 331–55. A study of the ways in which Wordsworth ("lake poet" and nineteenth-century, post-Enlightenment, socially conscious, educated European) deals with "social man" and of the relationship of his insights to concepts developed systematically in sociology.

WESTKOTT, MARCIA. "Conservative Method." *Philosophy of the Social Sciences* 7: 1 (March 1977): 67–76. Contends that the conservatism of modern sociology is not traceable so much to the theoretical tradition in sociology as to its conservative methodology, derived from Comte through K. Mannheim.

Index

Aron, Raymond: *Main Currents in Sociological Thought*, 121, 123, 124

Art, 127–153; and imagination, 127, 131–32, 135–37, 139–40, 142, 152–53; and moral function, 130–32, 144–45, 147–48, 149–50; and science, 131–32, 143–45, 151–53; as expression, 128–30, 131, 145; as idealization, 128, 130–32. 139, 145; as imitation, 128, 130–31, 145; as propaganda, 132, 135; education, 115–16, 132–33; medieval, 128–29; poetry, 133–34, 139, 141–42; structure, 140–42, 150–51

Babeuf, 33
Bacon, F., 86
Bellamy, Edward: *Looking Backward*, 145–47, 149
Berlin, Sir I., 154
Bernard, Claude, 143–44
Blake, William, 126, 155, 156, 158
Bliaux, Sophie, 26, 28, 104, 156
Bowman, Sylvia: *Edward Bellamy Abroad*, 146
Broussais, F. J. V., 52–54
Burdin, Dr., 31, 33

Cabanis, 42, 45
Capitalism, 119, 146–48, 156
Catholicism, 16, 24–25, 29, 48–49, 50–52, 103–104, 107, 112, 113, 123; Medieval, 82–85, 87–88, 101–103, 128–29, 132
Cerclet, M., 20–21
Chivalry, 82, 113, 119
Classification of the Sciences, 42, 46, 55, 57, 59–61, 68, 86, 95, 123, 127, 135, 155
Communism, 25, 114, 119, 145, 159n13

Comte, Alix, 16, 28
Comte, Auguste, chronology of life, 13–14; early years, 16–19; High Priest of Humanity, 15–16, 23, 27, 97, 110, 152, 157–58; "incomparable year" (with Clotilde de Vaux), 24, 97; lecturer / entrance examiner for École Polytechnique, 23–23; lectures / courses 26, 55–56, 93, 114; Marriage, 21–22; mental breakdown, 21–22, 52–53, 56; "mental hygiene" (hygiène cérébrale), 25, 30, 94, 159n14; Will and Secret Addition, 20, 22, 28; work with Saint-Simon, 19–20, 34–37

WORKS:
"Brief Estimate of Modern History," 39–40
Catéchisme, 24, 98–99
"Considerations on the Spiritual Power," 48–52
Cours (Positive Philosophy), 18, 21, 22–24, 41, 54, 56, 57–92, 127–30, 143–44
General View of Positivism, 93, 98–99, 127, 145
"Meditation," 18–19
"Philosophic Considerations on the Sciences and Savants," 21, 46–48
"Plan of the Scientific Operations Necessary for Reorganizing Society" ("Plan des travaux scientifiques . . ."), 20, 36, 40–46
"The Separation of Opinions from 'Aspirations,' " 38–39
Synthèse subjective, 25–26, 99, 127, 135–42
System of Positive Polity (Système de politique positive), 18, 24, 38, 46, 88, 91, 92, 93–126, 130–36, 151